First World War
and Army of Occupation
War Diary
France, Belgium and Germany

7 DIVISION
Divisional Troops
Royal Army Medical Corps
21 Field Ambulance
4 October 1914 - 30 November 1917

WO95/1647/1

The Naval & Military Press Ltd
www.nmarchive.com
Published in association with The National Archives

Published by

The Naval & Military Press Ltd

Unit 10 Ridgewood Industrial Park,

Uckfield, East Sussex,

TN22 5QE England

Tel: +44 (0) 1825 749494

www.naval-military-press.com

www.nmarchive.com

This diary has been reprinted in facsimile from the original. Any imperfections are inevitably reproduced and the quality may fall short of modern type and cartographic standards.

© Crown Copyright
Images reproduced by permission of The National Archives, London, England, 2015.

Contents

Document type	Place/Title	Date From	Date To
Heading	WO95/1647/1 7 Division (1) 21 Field Ambulance Sept 1914-Nov 1917		
Heading	7th Division 21st Field Ambulance Sep 1914-1917 Nov		
Heading	21st Field Amb		
War Diary	Lyndhurst Hants	14/09/1915	14/09/1915
Heading	21st Field Amb.		
War Diary		04/10/1914	06/10/1914
War Diary	Zeebrugge	07/10/1914	07/10/1914
War Diary	Bruges	08/10/1914	08/10/1914
War Diary	Breedene	09/10/1914	09/10/1914
War Diary	Bruges (S' Michael)	10/10/1914	10/10/1914
War Diary	Beernem	12/10/1914	12/10/1914
War Diary	Cools camp	13/10/1914	13/10/1914
War Diary	Roulers	14/10/1914	14/10/1914
War Diary	Ypres	15/10/1914	28/10/1914
War Diary	Halte	29/10/1914	29/10/1914
War Diary	Hooge	30/10/1914	31/10/1914
Miscellaneous	Battle of Ypres Tables Showing Sick & Wounded Dealt With By No.21 Field Ambulance	18/10/1914	18/10/1914
Heading	21st Field Amb.		
War Diary	Dickebusch	01/11/1914	01/11/1914
War Diary	Halte	02/11/1914	03/11/1914
War Diary	Ypres	03/11/1914	05/11/1914
War Diary	Locre	06/11/1914	06/11/1914
War Diary	Bailleul	07/11/1914	10/11/1914
War Diary	La Creche	11/11/1914	11/11/1914
War Diary	Bailleul	12/11/1914	15/11/1914
War Diary	Sailly	16/11/1914	19/11/1914
War Diary	Bac St. Maur	20/11/1914	30/11/1914
Heading	Dec 1914 21st Field Amb		
War Diary	Bau St Maur	02/12/1914	06/01/1915
Heading	121/4611 Jan 1915 Feb 1915 21st Field Ambulance Vol II		
War Diary	Bac St Maur	01/01/1915	28/02/1915
Heading	121/4896 March 1915 21st Field Ambulance Vol III		
War Diary	Bac St Maur	02/03/1915	02/03/1915
War Diary	Estaires	03/03/1915	31/03/1915
Miscellaneous	Statement of the Work of the 21st Field Ambulance During the Recent Attack on Neuve Chapelle	10/03/1915	10/03/1915
Miscellaneous	Table Showing Wounded Admitted To And Evacuated From Main Dressing Station No.21 Field Ambulance At College Horticulturale Rue Du College Estaires.		
Heading	121/5256 April 1915 21st Field Ambulance Vol IV		
War Diary	Estaires	01/04/1915	30/04/1915
Heading	21st Field Ambulance Vol V		
War Diary	Stazeele	02/05/1915	04/05/1915
War Diary	Estaires	05/05/1915	10/05/1915
War Diary	Bethune	11/05/1915	12/05/1915
War Diary	Essars	13/05/1915	19/05/1915
War Diary	Robecq	25/05/1915	31/05/1915

Type	Description	Start	End
Miscellaneous	Report On The Medical Transactions Of The 21st Field Ambulance during the active Period 9th & 10th May 1915	12/05/1915	12/05/1915
Miscellaneous	Report On The Medical Arrangements Of The Field Ambulance During The Period Of Activity Near La Quinque Rue	07/05/1915	07/05/1915
Miscellaneous	Statement of Cases Admitted to 21st Field Ambulance.		
Miscellaneous	No.21 Field Ambulance Return Showing Wounded Admitted And Evacuated During The Operation		
Heading	121/5993 4th Division 21st Field Ambulance Vol VI		
War Diary	Robecq	03/06/1915	09/06/1915
War Diary	Avelette	10/06/1915	30/06/1915
Miscellaneous	Report Of The Medical Arrangement Of The 21st Field Ambulance During The Period Of Activity Near Givenchy From 6 Pm 15th To 9am The 19th June 1915	19/06/1915	19/06/1915
Miscellaneous	Tables Shewing Wounded Admitted To And Evacuated From Main Dressing Station No.21 Field Ambulance Avelette		
Heading	121/6341 21st Field Ambulance Vol VII		
War Diary	Ham En Artois	01/07/1915	11/07/1915
War Diary	Zeslobes	12/07/1915	31/07/1915
Heading	7th Division 21st Field Ambulance Vol VIII From 1-31.8.15		
War Diary	Lannoy	01/08/1915	15/08/1915
War Diary	La Plouy Ferme	16/08/1915	27/08/1915
War Diary	Berguette	28/08/1915	31/08/1915
Heading	7th Division 21st Field Ambulance Vol IX Sept 15		
War Diary	Berguette	01/09/1915	03/09/1915
War Diary	Gonnehem	04/09/1915	24/09/1915
War Diary	Fouquieres	25/09/1915	25/09/1915
War Diary	La Bourse	25/09/1915	29/09/1915
War Diary	Bethune	30/09/1915	30/09/1915
Heading	7th Division 21st Field Ambulance Vol X Oct 15		
War Diary	Bethune	01/10/1915	16/10/1915
War Diary	Gonnehem	16/10/1915	17/10/1915
War Diary	St Hilaire	17/10/1915	22/10/1915
War Diary	Bethune	22/10/1915	31/10/1915
Heading	7th Division 21st Fd. Amb. Nov 1915 Vol XI		
War Diary	Bethune	01/11/1915	30/11/1915
Heading	7th Div F/130/1 21st Fd Amb. Dec Vol XII		
War Diary	Bethune	01/12/1915	02/12/1915
War Diary	Berguette	02/12/1915	06/12/1915
War Diary	Pont Remy	07/12/1915	07/12/1915
War Diary	Le. Mesge	07/12/1915	31/12/1915
Heading	7th Division F/130/2 21st Fd Amb Jan Vol XIII		
War Diary	Le Mesqe	02/01/1916	30/01/1916
War Diary	Cardonnette Corble	31/01/1916	31/01/1916
Heading	7th Div 21st Field Amb		
War Diary	Corble	01/02/1916	02/02/1916
War Diary	Sailly Laurette	02/02/1916	27/02/1916
Heading	21 Fd Amb Vol XV		
War Diary	Sailly	01/03/1916	01/03/1916
War Diary	Laurette	02/03/1916	07/03/1916
War Diary	Ribemont	08/03/1916	30/03/1916
War Diary	Corble	30/03/1916	30/03/1916
Heading	7th Division 21 F. Amb. April 1916		

War Diary	Corble	01/04/1916	27/04/1916
War Diary	Morlancourt	28/04/1916	29/04/1916
Heading	7th Div 21 F. Amb. May 1916		
War Diary	Bray-Corbie Road K21.D.8.9	01/05/1916	07/05/1916
War Diary	Morlancourt	08/05/1916	31/05/1916
Heading	7th Div No.21 Field Ambulance June 1916		
War Diary	Morlancourt	01/06/1916	30/06/1916
Miscellaneous	D.A.G. G.H.Q. 3rd Echelon	01/07/1916	01/07/1916
Heading	7th Division No. 21 Field Ambulance July 1916		
War Diary	Morlancourt	01/07/1916	21/07/1916
War Diary	Heilly	22/07/1916	31/07/1916
Heading	7th Div No.21 Field Ambulance Aug 1916		
War Diary	Heilly	01/08/1916	13/08/1916
War Diary	Ribemont	14/08/1916	31/08/1916
Heading	7th Division No. 21 F. A. Sept 1916 Oct 1916		
War Diary	Ribemont	01/09/1916	05/09/1916
War Diary	Buire	06/09/1916	13/09/1916
War Diary	Dours	14/09/1916	14/09/1916
War Diary	Crouy	15/09/1916	15/09/1916
War Diary	Huchenville	16/09/1916	16/09/1916
War Diary	Metern	18/09/1916	21/09/1916
War Diary	Nieppe	22/09/1916	21/10/1916
War Diary	B 16.c.6.6.	23/10/1916	31/10/1916
Heading	7th Div 21st Field Ambulance Nov 1916		
War Diary	Nieppe	01/11/1916	02/11/1916
War Diary	La Creche	03/11/1916	03/11/1916
War Diary	Metern	09/11/1916	09/11/1916
War Diary	Staple	10/11/1916	10/11/1916
War Diary	St Martin	11/11/1916	11/11/1916
War Diary	Eperlecques	15/12/1916	15/12/1916
War Diary	Pihem	16/11/1916	16/11/1916
War Diary	Cuhem	18/11/1916	18/11/1916
War Diary	Teneur	19/11/1916	19/11/1916
War Diary	Frevent	20/11/1915	20/11/1915
War Diary	Beauval	21/11/1916	21/11/1916
War Diary	Acheux	22/11/1916	23/11/1916
War Diary	Forceville	25/11/1916	25/11/1916
War Diary	Clairfaye	26/11/1916	29/11/1916
Heading	7th Div 21st Field Ambulance Dec 1916		
War Diary	Clairfaye	04/12/1916	06/12/1916
War Diary	Mailley Maillet	06/12/1916	30/12/1916
Heading	7th Div No.21 Field Ambulance Jan 1917		
War Diary	Mailley Maillet	02/01/1917	21/01/1917
War Diary	Val De Maison	21/01/1917	31/01/1917
Heading	7th Div No.21 Field Ambulance Feb 1917		
War Diary	Val De Maison	02/02/1917	21/02/1917
War Diary	Vauchelles	22/02/1917	28/02/1917
Heading	7th Div No.21 Field Ambulance Mar 1917		
War Diary	Vauchelles	01/03/1917	21/03/1917
War Diary	Bertrancourt	24/03/1917	24/03/1917
War Diary	Mailly Maillet Red House	25/03/1917	31/03/1917
Heading	7th Div No.21 F.A. April 1917		
War Diary	Red House Mailley-Maillet	03/04/1917	07/04/1917
War Diary	P 17.c.7.3	07/04/1917	11/04/1917
War Diary	Bucquoy 7.2d.5.5 A (57 D)	15/04/1917	30/04/1917
Heading	7th Div No. 21.f.a.		

War Diary	Bucquoy 7.28.A.5.5	02/05/1917	07/05/1917
War Diary	L'Abbaye Mory	07/05/1917	15/05/1917
War Diary	Bucquoy	16/05/1917	28/05/1917
Heading	No.21. F.A.		
War Diary	Bucquoy	02/06/1917	22/06/1917
War Diary	Ervillers	23/03/1917	27/06/1917
War Diary	Behagnies	28/06/1917	30/06/1917
Heading	No. 21. F.A July 1917		
War Diary	Behagnies	03/07/1917	30/07/1917
Heading	No.21 F.A. Aug 1917		
War Diary	Behagnies	03/08/1917	09/08/1917
War Diary	Bienvillers Au Bois	11/08/1917	25/08/1917
War Diary	Pommera	28/08/1917	29/08/1917
War Diary	Ouderdom (Sheet 28)	30/09/1917	30/09/1917
Heading	No.21 F.A Sept 1917		
War Diary	Duderdom	01/09/1917	01/09/1917
War Diary	Map.27. K.27.A.8.3.	02/09/1917	02/09/1917
War Diary	Map 27. N. 30.B.1.8	03/09/1917	08/09/1917
War Diary	Haut. Arques	13/09/1917	15/09/1917
War Diary	La Wattine	16/09/1917	27/09/1917
War Diary	Duve Wirquin	27/09/1917	27/09/1917
War Diary	St. Hubershoak	28/09/1917	30/09/1917
Heading	No. 21. F.A Oct 1917		
War Diary	Ypres Ecole De Bienfaisance Ypres Menin Road	01/10/1917	04/10/1917
War Diary	Ypres Ecole De Bienfaisance	05/10/1917	07/10/1917
War Diary	Ecole de Blenfaisanc Ypres-Menin Road	08/10/1917	11/10/1917
War Diary	Zevecoten	12/10/1917	18/10/1917
War Diary	Berthen	19/10/1917	24/10/1917
War Diary	N.6.a.8.8. Sheet 27.	29/10/1917	30/10/1917
War Diary	Ebblinghem	31/10/1917	31/10/1917
Heading	No.21 F.A.		
War Diary	Ebblinghem	01/11/1917	08/11/1917
War Diary	Ecquire	09/11/1917	09/11/1917
War Diary	Senlecques	10/11/1917	11/11/1917
War Diary	Ecquire	12/11/1917	12/11/1917
War Diary	Fruges	13/11/1917	13/11/1917
War Diary	Boyaval	14/11/1917	19/11/1917
War Diary	Legnago (Italy)	25/11/1917	25/11/1917
War Diary	Asigliano	26/11/1917	26/11/1917
War Diary	Campiglia	27/11/1917	27/11/1917
War Diary	Villaga	28/11/1917	29/11/1917
War Diary	Campodoro	30/11/1917	30/11/1917

WO 95/1647/1

7 Division

① 21 Field Ambulance

Sept 1914 – Nov 1917

*TH DIVISION

21ST FIELD AMBULANCE

SEP 1914 - ~~DEC 1918~~ (1917) NOV

To ITALY DEC 17

7.

21st Field Amb

Sept 19th

Army Form C. 2118.

WAR DIARY
or
INTELLIGENCE SUMMARY

(Erase heading not required.)

Instructions regarding War Diaries and Intelligence Summaries are contained in F. S. Regs., Part II. and the Staff Manual respectively. Title pages will be prepared in manuscript.

Hour, Date, Place	Summary of Events and Information	Remarks and references to Appendices
1914	Formed unit.	
14 Sept. — LYNDHURST, HANTS.	Started mobilizing 21st Field Ambulance. 160 men joined from depot at HOME ALDERSHOT. Medical equipt. had about arrived — Est.14	
18 Sept. — do.	The remainder of the personnel joined from Gibraltar, Malta & Japan including a proportion of NCOs but not to Scale of War Establisht. Officers consisting of 2 Special Reserve & gazetted on entry Major T. Phillips two Regular RAMC officer Major W.D. KELLY & Capt. T. Phillips also joined & posted to command B+C Sections respectively — Ent.14	

21st FIELD AMB.

Oct. 1914

Date	Place	Entry
4 Oct.	do.	Mobilization continues to date; Ordnance Equipment Stores drawn, a/c personnel + 2 Chaplains (1 C of E + 1 RC) joined (attached)
5 Oct.	do.	Mobilization completed — Inspected by G.O.C. Left Lymehurst at 6.15 a.m. — Embarked on H.T. "Australind" at SOUTHAMPTON between 1.30 & 4 p.m. — on march 2 horses sick (one strangles & one lame). Left Remount Docks under V.O. 2 substitutes from Remount Depot at Southampton Embarked on H.T. "Novarin" — E.M.
6 Oct.	↓	Sailed from SOUTHAMPTON at 7.30 p.m. arrived SANDOWN Bay at 9 a.m. — Orders to Ship's Master to proceed to DOVER & thence to ZEEBRUGGE — There were 4 men absent at Southampton. E.M.
7 Oct.	ZEEBRUGGE	Landed at 7 a.m. — finally disembarked at 7 p.m. & marched to BRUGES where we billeted at Cavalry Barracks
8 Oct.	BRUGES	Marched to BREEDENE near OSTEND in Billets. Absentees rejoined — from No 22 F. Amby who was "landed" at OSTEND
9 Oct.	BREEDENE	Marched to BRUGES at 4 p.m. arrived 12 midnight billeted near St. MICHAEL — E.M.

Army Form C. 2118.

WAR DIARY
or
INTELLIGENCE SUMMARY

(Erase heading not required.)

Instructions regarding War Diaries and Intelligence Summaries are contained in F. S. Regs., Part II. and the Staff Manual respectively. Title pages will be prepared in manuscript.

Hour, Date, Place	Summary of Events and Information	Remarks and references to Appendices
1914		
10th Oct. BRUGES (St Michael)	Marched to BEERNEM with part of 7th Div. - Remained in Billets here two nights.	
12 " BEERNEM.	Marched to COOLSCAMP. Billetted one night.	
13 " COOLSCAMP	Marched to ROULERS. Billetted 1 night. "B" Sect. got orders at Bulletinal BEERNEM (8 m. train)	
14 " ROULERS	Marched from "B" Sect. to YPRES. "B" Sect. regained	
15 " YPRES.	Tent Sub Sect. "B" opened Dressing Station at the Convent DES DAMES ROUS BRUGGE — Ent	
16. do	Under orders arms closed "B" opened "A" instead. "C" Sect. proceeded on 16th to HALTE on the YPRES-MENIN Road to form an Advanced Dressing Statn. The Bearer Sub Divn of BFD at the same time proceeding to the GOD 22nd Inf. Bde. in front of the point toward GHELUVELT. (NCO for clearing work Captain T. PHILLIPS in command of Advanced Dressing Station which proceeded from the Chateau S.E. of the YPRES-MENIN Rd near 7th kilometre mark. — Ent	
17 " do —	Tent Sub Div "B" proceeded with No 18 Adv Hospital to YPRES-MENIN Rd to take Ralean House to GHELUVELT & BECELARE - As a interment of the 7 Div hosp. was established onward to open me and open at the École MARIE RUE de LILLE. YPRES where on the 22/23rd 198 wounded Cavalries were dealt with & removed. "B" Tent Sub-Div in two lorries with "A" at the ROUS BRUGGE Convent. Ent	
27 do	Up to this date have been too busy to make Diary entries - a general enemies position has been held to that E. the 7th Div & 3rd Cavalry Div. fighting of a very severe nature has taken place in the 15th Dec. Large number of casualties amounting to 1820 have passed thro the main Dressing Station (2nd F.A. A.M.S. incl All Divisions) at YPRES to the Base having been evacuated by Ambulance Trains & motor Convoys - The number of recorded deaths = 40. Ent	See Appendix I. Table of Casualties for the period of the YPRES Battle attaches at end. Ent

WAR DIARY
or
INTELLIGENCE SUMMARY

(Erase heading not required.)

Army Form C. 2118.

Instructions regarding War Diaries and Intelligence Summaries are contained in F. S. Regs., Part II. and the Staff Manual respectively. Title pages will be prepared in manuscript.

Hour, Date, Place	Summary of Events and Information	Remarks and references to Appendices
28 Oct 1914. YPRES.	A very quiet day, evacuated 136 casualties by motor ambulances to HAZEBROUCK. 12 lying cases remain. — Made payments to party personnel — Evacuated the 12 lying down cases to Amb. Train No 24 Sunday order 7 sisters 7 Divs joined up with "C" Sect. Billetted in a Bungalow building 2 mile En.	
29th Oct — HALTE	Short of HALTE on the YPRES—MENIN Road — Dealt with 6 cases during the night, but none taken off waggons. Ordered forward by an MO Div to position more advanced recoomment to the main Road.	
30th Oct. HOOGE	Accordingly opened a Dressing Station ¾ in advance of "C" Section in the Village School of HOOGE. Where there were 10 Regular beds. 1 four wards. Supply however though meagre we in order. Examined & dealt with 37 cases of wounded during the night — 1 "C" Sect. These continues had Br. of Ew	
31st Oct. do	Owing to heavy shellfire & retirement of troops we ordered by GOC 1st Cops to close station — This was done in good order without any casualties — ordered by GOC 1st Cops to park at DICKEBUSCH — Started night in Old Brewery there. Also 400 Bearer Subdiv' into Ambulance waggons remained at HALTE — YPRES—MENIN Rd. They collected wounded about HO, & sent some to Hospitals at YPRES direct — Ent	

BATTLE OF YPRES

TABLES SHOWING SICK & WOUNDED DEALT WITH BY No. 21 FIELD AMBULANCE

OCT. 18th TO NOV. 4th 1914

TABLE No. I

	VII DIVISION				3rd CAVALRY DIVISION				OTHER CORPS				FRENCH ARMY				GERMAN ARMY				BELGIANS				TOTAL	
	SICK		WOUNDED		SICK		WOUNDED		SICK		WOUNDED		SICK		WOUNDED		SICK		WOUNDED		SICK		WOUNDED		SICK	WOUNDED
	OFFICERS	OTH.RKS	OFFICERS	OTH.RKS	OFFICERS	OTH.RKS	OFFICERS	OTH.RKS	OFFICERS	OTH.RKS	OFFICERS	OTH.RKS	OFFICERS	OTH.RKS	OFFICERS	OTH.RKS	OFFICERS	OTH.RKS	OFFICERS	OTH.RKS	OFFICERS	OTH.RKS	OFFICERS	OTH.RKS		
	13	320	54	1243	10	61	15	120	2	50	NIL	93	NIL	1	NIL	9	NIL	NIL	1	14	NIL	NIL	NIL	1	457	1553

TABLE No. II

WOUNDED			
UNITS	OFFICERS	OTH.RKS	TOTAL
VII Division	54	1243	1297
III Cav Bde	15	120	135
Other Corps	NIL	93	93
French Army	"	9	9
German Army	1	14	15
Belgians	NIL	1	1
TOTAL	40	1483	1553

TABLE No. III

SICK			
UNITS	OFFICERS	OTH RANKS	TOTAL
VII Division	13	320	333
III Cav Bde	10	61	71
Other Corps	2	50	52
French Army	"	1	1
German Army	"	"	-
Belgians	"	"	-
TOTAL	25	432	457

TABLE No. IV

DEATHS			
UNITS	OFFICERS	OTH.RANKS	TOTAL
VII Division	6	26	32
III Cav Bde	1	6	7
Other Corps	NIL	2	2
French Army	NIL	2	2
German Army	1	NIL	1
Belgians	NIL	1	1
TOTAL	8	37	45

TABLE No. V

RECAPITULATION			
	OFFICERS	OTH RANKS	TOTAL
WOUNDED	40	1483	1553
SICK	25	432	457
TOTAL	95	1915	2010

Note - 9/10ths of the above cases were dealt with during the period 18/10/14 to 28/10/14 when two Sections of the Fd. Amb. Tent Sub-Divns. formed the main dressing station of the 7th Divn & 3rd Cavalry Divn.

E. St. J. K. Nasmith
Major
O.C. 21 F. Amb.

21st Field Amb.

Nov. 1914

1 Nov. SCHREBUSCH

2 Nov. HAZTE.

— marched to HAZTE & found advance Rwng Station Beaver party) in Farm there for the night. Some heavy shells fell closely & there are Corporain from our own heavy guns shelled windows — 42 Coves were dealt with during the night.

Some heavy shelling again a few yards off, several Shrapnel dealt with in the morning. The opposing shells returned by Reg Gun. So does a Station sparks Sam at HOTEL Farm hard by. 12:30 p.m. coms again in Henry Gun fire occurred of with fire all round there was no

Forces C 2118/15 y
1247 W 8299 200,000 (E) 8/14 J.B.C. & A.

WAR DIARY
or
INTELLIGENCE SUMMARY
(Erase heading not required.)

Army Form C. 2118.

Hour, Date, Place	Summary of Events and Information	Remarks and references to Appendices
1914	and escort of 1 Corp & R.Dr. gunte etc.	
3 Nov - HALTE	At 1 am Lt Richardson R.H.A. "C" Sqdn was killed by shell. Captain Phillip Raine severely wounded, 16 coy reqd Rame attacked 2 wds etc. and a.s.c. driver slightly wounded received man (15) of Regt Transport picked up & put on ambulance wagons & taken into Field close by wounded - all put on ambulance wagons & taken into Field F. Ambulance. to YPRES Grand Place where men were put in the Cloth Hall. 1st waggons parked in the Grand Place. Canadian & new Foundland Fire Brigade Stations ordered by AT. 8 S.W. Again 1st Corps opened in Rooms above Moyenne Subsequently ordered by HQ R.F.A. 2nd Corps opened in rooms above Rue de BRUCHE. Did so at 2.30 pm. Heavy shelling occured in daylight. Remained day & night at intervals. Sent out 3 waggons to the Bavers to	
do BIVOUAC YPRES	HOOGE 5 to brought in 17 wounded - Grenadiers wounded to POPPERINGHE by motor ambulance &	
4. Nov. do	received yeomanry & 1st Coys to pack up to move - Ambulances & some A.S.C. Coys to be ready to move - O.S.M & A.S.C. pharmacy at 1.30 pm to orders - moved to park at DICKEBUSCH - Did so - Arrived at DICKEBUSCH - but front part difficult to find - a Billet in the rain - all places near by taken by the French Troops who were in any numbers finally got some poor accomodation at CYPER CLAEYS farm about 1 kilometre up the road on the right, just past the 4 kilometre mark on the YPRES - DICKEBUSCH Rd.	
5th Nov.	Buried Lt A. SOUTHGATE of the 2nd Yorks Regt at back of CLAEYS farm whose body has been carried from YPRES. Transfers 2 wounded Civilians to Burgomaster Hospital at DICKEBUSCH - Recd orders from AT of 7 D.S. to LOCRE to come under orders of B.O.C. 21st Inf B & Repo to march independently. PM marched 7.15 pm reached Billet 1 mile NOT LOCRE at 12 PM instanu	

WAR DIARY
or
INTELLIGENCE SUMMARY
(Erase heading not required.)

Army Form C. 2118

Instructions regarding War Diaries and Intelligence Summaries are contained in F. S. Regs, Part II. and the Staff Manual respectively. Title pages will be prepared in manuscript.

Hour, Date, Place	Summary of Events and Information	Remarks and references to Appendices
1914. 6 Nov. LOCRE.	2nd Inf. Bde. & other 7 Div. Troops arrived at 8.30 a.m. — Reported to Gen. T. Gore at 9/1st Bn. No orders until 11 a.m. when I was directed to/toward Billets & Officers toward to BAILLEUL. Roads & tracks much. Three no. 2 at 1.30 p.m. marched at 2 p.m. for BAILLEUL. Road congested, frost 15 miles in 4 hours! Arrived at Baillé & Puttes in inmate asylum Stables at 8 p.m. Wrote Mrs. Richardson & next of kin of Capt. Phillips. No orders up to 1 p.m.	Err
7 Nov. Bailleul.	Obtained several pairs of Boots from Ordnance (Div.) for personnel requiring Country Boots. Shift of "C" Section — Parades & inspection.	Err
8 Nov. do	Horse lit. inspect — There were many injuries sustained when shelled out at HAUTE & HOOGE & by Beaver & in firing line at Beaver. at YPRES — 25 Sick received from 21st Inf. Bde & Brigades H.Q. Casualty Hospital ordered towards PLOEGSTEERT by a.m. 9.	Err
	2nd Inf. Bde. who had already joined there — Billeted at BERTOUX's farm 150 yards N. of BAILLEUL – MENENTIERES Rt immediately N. of village of LA CRECHE — Could not open Dressing station as no decampment could be found — Nos. 1 & 2 Amb. Sgts. occupied any available hut on Sot. Sent forward 2 Amb. wagons & 2 Bearers under Cie André to find billets short of PLOEGSTEERT & report to a.m. 2nd Inf. Bde.	Err
10 Nov. do	Said personnel: Major Kelly, proceeded to POPPERINGHE for dental treatment. Lt. Col. O'Reilly Rama joined from No. 12 Gen. Hosp. ROUEN. Parties E"C" Section. Beaver to Bn. D'Ur. Lt. Argo proved efforts to "B" Beaver sub D'Ur. Opened Dressing Station on main road near Farm with the Beav. Est. Sub Dir — Rec'd. 8 Sich & 44 Casualties — Sut Farm & Baillent Clemy. Hosp.	Err

WAR DIARY
or
INTELLIGENCE SUMMARY
(Erase heading not required.)

Army Form C. 2118.

Hour, Date, Place	Summary of Events and Information	Remarks and references to Appendices
1914		
11 Nov LA CRECHE.	Sent "B" Recve Sub Div & 3 fresh ambulances to relieve 2 Recves near PLOEGSTEERT. Received truce with arms in interior. Hour 50.c 21.30. 2nd Fd Bde who have present away & will hold good. Note further orders.	
12 Nov BAILLEUL	Left CRECHE. Billeted at Brewery premises E of BAILLEUL. Lt. STAFFORD & Lt. CHRISTIE rejoined unit. unit for duty.	
13 " "	Remained in same billets	
14 " "	Marched with 21st Infy Bde towards Bac St Maur but returned until 13th same day to BAILLEUL	
15 " "	Remained at Brewery premises at Bailleul — weather very wet.	
16 " SAILLY	Marched with 21st Infy Bde towards SAILLY & billeted at MARECHAL FARM 600 yards N of Pt. TOURNIQUT, SAILLY.	
17 " "	Arranged with G.O.C 21st Infy Bde to send Bearers of this Sub Divn to point 800 yds NNE of Bac St Maur to form 1 NCO & 2 Nursing orderlies & 1 "B" Eqpt. Formed Tent & Forage Cart of B 1 NCO + 2 Nursing orderlies SE of Bac St Maur to form Advance Dressing Station under Lt. JARDINE. Communn to position about 2 kilometers & & "Tent Sub-Division to points along stream flowing N of SAILLY near Cross Roads. Established Small Dressing Station + Hospl with a "Tent Sub-Div" at MARECHAL FARM. Godyards No 26 (Beary Hope).	Eur.
18th Nov "	8 cases. 1 wounded admitted. 1 wounded Q.a.c (G.S. Hand).	
19 Nov "	1 wounded case (G.S. Hand).	
20 Nov BAC ST MAUR.	Moved from Hd Qrs Dr. & furn to premises in Farm (BARBRY'S) at BAC ST MAUR. — no casualties. 2 sick evacuated.	
21 " "	"C" Sect Tent Sub Divn took over School premises 300 yds E on SE side of SAILLY — ARMENTIERE Rd. — the Sisters. Lamps recommnd. Jun 140 - 268 cases.	Eur.

1247 W 3289 200,000 (E) 8/14 J.B.C.&A. Forms C. 2118/11.

Army Form C. 2118.

WAR DIARY
or
INTELLIGENCE SUMMARY

(Erase heading not required.)

Instructions regarding War Diaries and Intelligence Summaries are contained in F. S. Regs., Part II. and the Staff Manual respectively. Title pages will be prepared in manuscript.

Hour, Date, Place	Summary of Events and Information	Remarks and references to Appendices
1914. 22 nov. Bac S. Maur.	Lt Buthen inspected Bde Reserve Billets at me.	
24 "	Lt CHRISTIE left for Div.l Train mus. Charge.	
26 "	L. Griffin joined unit this day.	
" "	Lt Quenlan ditto	
30 "	Major Kelly rejoined. Lt Griffin transferred to hv.t Charge Queenlan	
" "	Lt Quenlan to transport charge XXIII Bde RFA	

21st FIELD AMB

DEC 1914

Confidential.

War Diary

of

21st Field Ambulance

From 14th Sept 1914 To 6th Jany 1915

Volume I

2 Decr	BAD ST MAUR.	Lt Stafford to Brigade charge. 2 Bed ford Rgt & Lt Ruan to 7 days leave. Rendered Special Report to arms? Our of work of certain officers men of the unit at the Battle of YPRES? Lt Button relieved Lt Ingram in temporary charge of 2 Scots Fus?. & Henry 8th Rfles. Lt Lukas "
7 Decr	"	Lt Argo returned from 7 days leave to England
9 Decr	"	Lt Maur "
10 Decr	"	Lt Quinlan rejoined
18 Decr	"	Lt Stafford reported – S.of the LYS – 2nd 18 Dis noteneye but 22nd 23rd? A General attack 19/12/14 to 21/12/14. 106 cases 2nd Sick of Div – admitted during fever a hard trecking 1000 yards N of 82 wounded – Further purpose a hard trecking 1000 yards N of "C" Scts. was taken into use. Evacuated to Clearing Hosp. MERVILLE.
23 Decr	"	Lt Argo sent Seh. to MERVILLE suffering from Neurasthenia Insomnia – Lt Fowler joined in Scots. 1st Grenadier Guards
25 Decr	"	Lt Stafford to Temporary Charge of 2 Rgt Warwicks Cap.n Wright
29 Decr	"	Lt Burton selected for charge of 2 Rgt Warwicks arrived to replace him
1915 6 Jany	"	Lt Fowler proceeded to temporary Charge of 2/Yorkshire Rgt –

21st Field Ambulance

Vol II

WAR DIARY or INTELLIGENCE SUMMARY

Army Form C. 2118.

(Erase heading not required.)

Instructions regarding War Diaries and Intelligence Summaries are contained in F.S. Regs., Part II. and the Staff Manual respectively. Title pages will be prepared in manuscript.

Hour, Date, Place	Summary of Events and Information	Remarks and references to Appendices
1915. January. Bac St Maur.	Capt. Cartwright-Reeve who joined 3rd Bn Batt in place of Lt Sutton from Ref. charge of 7 wounded, has been posted to Command of "C" section. Application by self for 7 days leave to England granted.	
7 Jany do.	Proceeded on leave to England – Major W.D. Kelly of in command.	
14 " "	Returned from leave – resumed command. 7 N.C.Os & Men (of HQrs Platoon). The weather has been very wet & found where HQrs floors), due there has been a daily average of 2 wounded casualties, due to snipers recurring generally on the occasions Bn is relieving from trenches.	
15 " do	Several men of unit admit having some body lice – inspected Billets thoroughly damaged & have their blankets & clothing kit inspected. Advanced dressing station Sunday – also Lt Col's B Co. Back Home meeting rooms at Fleur Baix – which has been found in the Brewery premises there & is under the supervision of Lt Jardine Senr. – Several dryers' rooms & feet rubbing rooms established in these billets with a permanent detachment of 1 to 6 men RAMC (Bearers) in each.	
16 Jany do.	Snow fell – Lt Huckersham & Major Kelly RTR ill with Influenza. The Tonvrierz generally present in men of unit now well in hand – No Serious cases – have returned	

WAR DIARY or INTELLIGENCE SUMMARY

Army Form C. 2118.

(Erase heading not required.)

Hour, Date, Place	Summary of Events and Information	Remarks and references to Appendices
1915 - Bac St Maur:	all blankets in use in Hospital - amongst personnel all wearing apparel - This includes adv: dressing station - Since	
16 Jany (cont'd) do	weather both have been obtained the trenches has decreased.	
23 Jany - do	Lt Jardine & Lt Stafford proceeded on 7 days leave to England	
30 Jany - do	Lt Stafford to Temporary in Charge of 35 B/RFA	
" " do	Lt Quinlan to Temporary charge of 2/ Gordons	
" - do	Snow first for past 2 days now melting	
" - do	To Divl Reserve Billets near Rue la Cyse to obtain further set of drying rooms - one only found accommodates for -	
31 " do	The past month has been singularly free from any incidence of casualties in trenches -	

E.C. Hayes
Major RAMC
OC 2/1st Field Amb Ca

Army Form C. 2118.

WAR DIARY
or
INTELLIGENCE SUMMARY

(Erase heading not required.)

Instructions regarding War Diaries and Intelligence Summaries are contained in F. S. Regs., Part II. and the Staff Manual respectively. Title pages will be prepared in manuscript.

Hour, Date, Place	Summary of Events and Information	Remarks and references to Appendices
1915 1 Feb. Bac St Maur	Lt. E.S. Miller (Temp RAMC) joined from New Zeal'd Hospital.	
2 do	Short cold weather. — Reported to OC No 8 7 Div'l S that the troops are getting tinned salmon too frequently (4 times last week) Hansen & Jan. James'll gof sat. interria. Yesterday Acting Sgt. Kirk joined 1/SR Staffords as acting 2nd Lt. on probation.	
6 Feb do —	Lt. Stafford & Quinlan rejoined on the 6 & 7th inst respectively. On the 7th Lt. Nash took temporary charge of 2 Rhondda's & F. Ambulance in charge of the 2 Rhondda's. S/Major Fitch proceeds to RAMC Depot on promotion to Lt. &QMaster	
11 Feb. do	Saw Norris & successor. — Lt. Quinlan yesterday proceeded to temporary rest change "Yoe" 7 Div'l Ammun: Col'n returning to Bay	
12 Feb — do	ordered by ADMS to detail a M.O. for temporary relief of M.S/c S/R Scots from 16.2.22 inst (Lt. Snary) —	
14 Feb — do	ADMS 7 Div'll posted Lt. E.S. Miller to temporary charge 2/Wilts vice Lt. Forster who proceeds to No 22 F Ambce	
16 Feb. do do — do	Lt. Quinlan to 7 days leave QM S/A. Holford from No.5 F. Ambce to replace S/Major Mulcahy as acting Sergt Major	

Army Form C. 2118.

WAR DIARY
or
INTELLIGENCE SUMMARY
(Erase heading not required.)

Instructions regarding War Diaries and Intelligence Summaries are contained in F.S. Regs., Part II. and the Staff Manual respectively. Title pages will be prepared in manuscript.

Hour, Date, Place	Summary of Events and Information	Remarks and references to Appendices
1915. Bac St Maur R. 21.Feb	Lt E.C. Linton (Empty St Pierre) joined from Rouen 19/1/15 vice Lt. Forbes permanently transferred to No 22 F. Amb.	
22. do	Major Hetherelly to 7 days leave to England.	
23. do	Lt. Quinlan rejoined from leave.	
28. do	During the past month there have been no warlike engagements. The 1st & 21st Infy Bde to which this ambulance is attached holding the trenches in relief of 3 days each. There have been a few casualties average 2 per diem for month. The incidence of sickness has been will below the usual. 3 per thousand little or no foot trouble has occurred.	

E.C.Taylor
Major RAMC
OC 21st F.Amb.

121/4896 7 Avis

121/4896
March 1915

21st Field Amb Balance

Vol III

S1

WAR DIARY
or
INTELLIGENCE SUMMARY

Army Form C. 2118.

Hour, Date, Place	Summary of Events and Information	Remarks and references to Appendices
1915.		
2nd March Bac S. Maur.	Major R.D. Kelly returned from leave to England – Made reconnaissance of premises College Hortaillries ESTAIRE with A.D.M.S. 7 Divn as to its suitability for use as No 21 Field Ambulance – Left Bac S. Maur with the whole of No 21 F.A. & opened up same at the College Hortaillries ESTAIRE – The affiliated 126 of Infantry Bg No 21 being in Billets close by.	
3rd March ESTAIRES	I have been promoted Lt.Col. myself with effect from 1st inst – vide London Gazette of 1/3/15.	
4 March do	Conference with Regimental M.O.'s of 21st Infantry Bde re sick & sanitary arrangements.	
8 March do	Informed by A.D.M.S. 7 Divn of proposed attack on German position times from 10 to 10½ – We understand we to arrange for rest of casualties of 21st Bde to F.O. Adv. – Saw G.O.C. 21 Infantry openly.	
9 do do	Saw G.O.C. again today. He approved of turning for an advanced Dressing Station – He also approved tonight for Rd. Coll. D.S. being in Reserve funds with London Highlanders – Established Advanced Dressing Station at LAVENTIE	
10 do do	At 12 o'c Germans ultimately to bombard on right flank down Communications where I remained most of the afternoon – being at LAVENTIE early that 7 Div Mounted attacked morning right very heavy day's work to ESTAIRE (main Dressing Station No 21 F.A.) Total received 7-9 pm 123 – Heavy Shrapnel perforated Christ collector Lt. all known casualties got in by 10 p.m – 1 PTE. RAINE killed + 4 wounded of No 21 F.A. Bearers Returned to ESDA. via LAVENTIE	

Army Form C. 2118.

WAR DIARY
or
INTELLIGENCE SUMMARY
(Erase heading not required.)

Instructions regarding War Diaries and Intelligence Summaries are contained in F. S. Regs., Part II. and the Staff Manual respectively. Title pages will be prepared in manuscript.

Hour, Date, Place	Summary of Events and Information	Remarks and references to Appendices
1915		
11 March – ESTAIRES	To Laventie – 14 cases had arrived by night. – To Beware Lane and Post. Took Lt Jardine self in Motor Ambulance waggon to FORT LOGY on L'ESTAIRE – LA BASSÉE Rd to see if the 2nd Bn[?] of the wounded could be evacuated that way. – That can't be done there afoot an old room near there Capture Trench. – Sent 6 Bearers under 2 Linton then tat up to 10pm FORT LOGY being hourly shelled no one were allowed up. L. O. Daily proceeded to M.23 6 operated to M'R "Beware".	Shell wounds 28/89 Rifle Major 36 Belgium – Civilians.
12 March do	A large number of wounded came thro' during the night from the 7th & 6th Indian Divisions (from 4pm 11th to 4pm 12th) walking wounded = 79 Sick + 110 officers + 110 officers 7.20 Left 7th Main Dressing Station at LAVENTIE (damage) with Bearer officers for night services & wounded of 2nd & 3rd Bgds 6th who left I'm Most Coys of 2nd Regs to yesterday. Lt. S. MATTHEW. Raid & Iron Bon Cognac near St Omer in Collecting Station in the Rue Cannon (M.22.a) shelled at 7am. – 1 Severe Casulties amongst "C" Section Bearers evacuated.	do
13 do do	To the S.E. Dies. 17 Bearers evacuated mostly during past 24 hrs. 1100 cases principally from M.34.c, M.29.c, 35.a + 34.9 as far as the front line to the York Trenches. Visited Advanced Dressing Stn LAVENTIE.	do
14 do do	Lt. Jam. D. Sutti MANC (S.R.) joined for duty from DIEPPE From 9pm 13/14/15 + pm 14/15 Cases, 3 officers 463 Other Ranks.	

Army Form C. 2118.

WAR DIARY
or
INTELLIGENCE SUMMARY

(Erase heading not required.)

Instructions regarding War Diaries and Intelligence Summaries are contained in F. S. Regs., Part II. and the Staff Manual respectively. Title pages will be prepared in manuscript.

Hour, Date, Place	Summary of Events and Information	Remarks and references to Appendices
1915 March 15 ESTAIRES	Light remained 12 hours last night – Saw DOC 21 Inf FA & utty at LAVENTIE. Arranged Stretcher Bearers from Gamow Lane, Rouge I Section at LAVENTIE for the present. "A" & "C" ESTAIRES. 21st Infy Bde have been withdrawn from the Trenches.	appendix 4 I.a (trois)
16. do	LAVENTIE – The recent action appears to have ended. The annexed Table shows the numbers & character of wounded & casualties passed thro' this this Ambulance during the period of this recent attack. There were large numbers of cases admitted (my due to exposure in Trenches more last 40 days) (Col. 268 &up 25). 5 are 3 cases. The Motorlanis has now been completely evacuated. Rendered Special Report of recommended situation (invalidation) of work of 21 FA in recent operations. Copy report annexed –	do
17. do	DDMS 1st Army inspected hospl. The Ambulance.	
18. do	At a Satire Plane is employ May of 7 Div. RE incl. Lt. Bulley all killed as at 5.30 am this morning 24 Benes at Front to under N.O'Reilly & ambulance proceeded to Rue Bacquart for clearing of casuals, 1 2nd Infy Bde who occupied Trenches last night.	
23. do		
24. do	To LAVENTIE 4.00 today evening, Saw 21st Infy Bde responsible position & cannot. During a. Interval which attack, advanced & gain'd 400 yds – Saw reason orders – Nothing left of	
26. do		
29. do	Boyd to fin Core. The probability of occupying some trenches. A VAC Station St Due – Bearers unknown from advance dressing station.	
31. do	21. Inf. FA. by relieves in the Trenches by 20 S/15/80. They go to bivouac at LA GORGE. N. ESTAIRES.	

E. C. Hayes RAMC
Lt Col RAMC
O.C. 21st Field Ambulance

(3)

1247 W 3299 200,000 (E) 8/14 J.B.C. & A. Forms/C. 2118/11.

Reference Map
Belgium Sheet 36
1 in 40,000

Statement of the work of the 21st Field Ambulance during the recent attack on NEUVE CHAPELLE 10th to 14th March 1915

The 21st Field Ambulance Tent Sub Divns of 'A' & 'C' Sections were already open at the Collège Horticultural ESTAIRES. Here there was accommodation for about 300 cases but the lying down accommodation was limited on account of the difficulty of getting stretchers upstairs, although the bannisters were sawn away for that purpose. There were 2 Dressing Rooms opened with 2 tables in each, so that 4 medical officers could work at the same time. There was a large receiving room which held 25 cases and as the number of wounded increased, the Father Superior placed 3 further ground floor rooms at my disposal as well as permitted the use of a large kitchen on the ground floor for the preparation of tea, soup and refreshments for the patients.

The A.D.M.S 7th Divn informed me on the 8th inst. of the proposed attack and in general the proposed movements of the 21st Inf Bde therein. He directed me to get in touch with the Bde. f.O.C. I saw the latter the same afternoon. He approved of my arrangement to establish an Advanced Dressing Station at LAVENTIE in the Patronage du Sacré Coeur M4 (5x5) where there was accommodation for 80 cases in straw, a dressing Room stretcher as well as Billets for the Bearers. A large yard behind the building accommodated 7 Horsed Ambulance Wagons

The advanced Dressing Station was accordingly opened here on the evening of the 8th inst.

It was formed from B Tent Sub Divn as follows:—

Personnel — 1 M.O.
1 Cpl
1 Cook
2 Nursing Orderlies

Equipment — Forage Cart with contents
Water Cart.

There are 3 Motor Ambulance Wagons attached to this unit & 1 was kept down at the Advanced Dressing Station for duty that night

(1)

2.

I saw the 21st Inf Bde Staff on the 9th March to make further arrangements for medical relief in the attack & also met the M.O's of the Regimental Units — 1 Bearer was attached to each M.O. to bring back information as to the position of the 1st groups of Casualties & the proposed 2nd Advanced Dressing Station indicated to them.

The f.O.C. 21 Infy Bde could give accommodation in the Reserve Trenches, where the Bde was massed for the attack for only 1 Stretcher SubDivn in the first instance — Lt. C.J. O'Reilly RAMC & B. Bearer Subdivn performed this duty.

The Roads &c routes were reconnoitred by my 3 Bearer Officers and myself the same day and it was arranged that one of the farms at M22a should be occupied as a 2nd Advanced Dressing Station as soon as the troops moved out to the attack.

10th March

On the morning of the ~~attack~~ 10th inst. the attack developed at 7.30 A.M. the 21st Infy Bde advancing over the ground M28 occupied the trenches vacated by the 28th Infy Bde deployed to the left over the ground M29 — In the advance 2 of the bearers attached to Regl M.O's were wounded but were able to indicate M28 D (N.W) as a spot where wounded lay.

20 odd cases were brought into the 2nd Advd Dressing Stn M22A by B Sub Divn Bearers, but there was heavy shrapnel fire when they were making a second effort & 1 man of the Bearers was killed & 1 wounded. Direct clearance immediately behind the troops was impracticable from this side during daylight.

I brought down the bearers of C Sub divn to the 2nd Advd Dressing Station at M22 A in the afternoon to be ready for clearance work that night — Shortly afterwards we got into direct communication with the M.O's 2 Bedes 24/nts & 2 Wilts & a few walking cases came in later by the road across M23 to a farm at the N end of the same road M23a. The Bearer Sub Divns B & C were out during the night & brought in by dawn over 100 cases.

11th March

In the early part of the day there was heavy shrapnel fire over the area M22, 23 & 29. As work was impossible from this side I went down with Lt Jardine RAMC of A Bearer Subdivn to PONT LOGY (M34C) where I met the

The ADMS 7th Divn & the Rue Tillaloy was reconnoitred up to M20(5x5) - A room in a dismantled house was selected at M20.B as a dressing station for C Bearers but Divn under Lt E.C Hunton R.A.M.C who was thereupon installed therein. About 30 cases during the day were collected from aid posts of 2nd Beds, West Yorks at haystacks M28D and were evacuated to PONT LOGY. The bombardment of the whole area & the ESTAIRES – LA BASSEE Rd up to the ROUGE CROIX was however great. During the night a large number of casualties from 7th & 8th Divns were collected from M29 B.C. D) where they lay in groups & similarly brought to PONT LOGY. Under orders of A.D.M.S. 7th Divn all my motor & horsed ambulance wagons took cases from PONT LOGY direct to main dressing Stn at ESTAIRES, though as the day before about a dozen walking cases came by the diagonal Road across M23 to 2nd Advanced Dressing Station at M22a & thence to 1st Advd Dressing Station LAVENTIE. From whence they were evacuated to ESTAIRES

The Bearers got in direct touch with the Regtl Aid posts at the Haystacks before mentioned
Lt Jardine R.A.M.C with remainder of Bearers at 11 p.m. moved down to PONT LOGY – Owing to the crush of transport along RUE TILLALOY half these Bearers were cut-off and remained at the large Barn at the Y Road Junction there PONT LOGY dressing cases and evacuating them from Rue Tillaloy into Motor ambulances to ESTAIRES. – Exact number of cases unknown. The remainder of the Bearers continued on and evacuated cases in M24 B & D & M35 A collecting 2 Beds from Regtl Aid Post in M35 a.

12th March.

At 7 a.m. in the morning the 2nd Advanced Dressing Stn at Farm M22a was struck by shell fire. There were 4 casualties amongst the Bearers (one severe abdominal) The Bearers were withdrawn to the 12th Advanced Dressing Station at LAVENTIE for a rest during the day, practical collection of wounded being out of the question – At dusk however, the shelling having abated the 3 Bearer Sub Divns returned and proceeded via the RUE TILLALOY & cleared to PONT LOGY, where the motor and horsed Ambulance wagons rendezvoused. Roughly 400 cases. The casualties were from 7th & 8th & Indian Divns & collected from aid posts at

M24C, M29C, M35a, M34B. up to as far as the front line of 2 Yorks Trenches. They were sent direct to the main dressing station of N⁰ 21 F.A.; who that night also received the overflow of the other Field Ambulances of 7th + 8th Divns.

13th March.

One section Sent to w. Bearers resting at 1st Advanced Dressing Station at LAVENTIE, other 2 billetted at Farm M22a little or no work being done during day time - Overnight wounded had been brought to Bde Hd Qrs Haystack M29a from 2 Wilts 2 Yorks + 2 R.S. Fusiliers by Regt Stretcher bearers + a second batch from R.S. Fus + 2 Wilts to road junction M29C. The 2 Beds evacuated to M35a (old German trenches) There was great shortage of Regt. Stretcher Bearers ? by casualty. The ambulance bearers evacuated these cases to PONT LOGY whence they were taken direct by motor Ambulance to main Dressing Station 21st F.A. at ESTAIRES.

14th March.

On the morning of the 14th inst. orderlies were sent to all Regt. M.O's The wounded were collected from the aid posts already mentioned they were then removed to PONT LOGY. The same aid posts were again visited that night + 11 cases were removed from M29 d Road junction.

It will thus be seen that nearly all the casualties especially lying cases, were sent 1st from the aid posts mentioned above to the PONT LOGY + thence direct by motor ambulance waggons of many different units (including 10 from the 2 Cavalry Divn which had been requisitioned for the purpose by the A.D.M.S. 7th Divn.) to the main Dressing Station of N⁰ 21 F.A. at ESTAIRES. All my horsed amb⁻ waggons shared in this duty in addition -

The casualties were nearly all redressed without exception and given antitetanic serum at the main dressing station at ESTAIRES. They were evacuated the following day mainly by N⁰ 2 Motor Convoy to Casualty Clearing Stations at MERVILLE; but on the night of the 12/13th

(In addition 2 ambulance trains were availed of) evacuation to LA GORGUE Station where the trains were in waiting was by motor ambulance wagons but on one occasion afternoon of 13th March 5 G.S. wagons from 7th Div Train took some 60 sitting cases to an interposed train also at LA GORGUE.

It will be seen that the position of the 1st Advance Dressing Station remained unaltered during the operations & had not much work to perform except as a parking place for the Horsed Ambulance Waggons & a resting place for the bearer Sub-Division personnel. If the advance had been greater it would have had fuller functions to perform being on the direct road of evacuation from AUBERS.

It will be moreover noticed that owing to the nature of the fighting with few exceptions the formation of regular Regtl. Aid Posts was impracticable, the wounded having to be collected into groups at the places indicated in the above report. The annexed table shows the numbers of wounded received by No 21 Field Ambulance distinguishing officers other ranks & enemy's wounded from 9 pm to 9 am daily as requested and differentiating Rifle from Artillery fire.

The number of wounded who died in this ambulance during the period in question was 10 (3 officers, 7 other ranks)

I have to thank the O.C. 1/3rd Field Ambce N. Mid. Division for the help of 3 of his officers who aided my tent Sub-Division personnel in dressing cases — also the M.O. 7th Div Train & Div Ammn Column for similar services at different periods during the heavy stress of the past 4 days.

No statement has been submitted by me to the G.O.C. B (?) Bde.

Signed E. C. Hayes
Lt Col RAMC
O.C. 21st Fd Ambce

17th March 1915

TABLES SHOWING WOUNDED ADMITTED TO AND EVACUATED FROM MAIN DRESSING STATION No. 21 FIELD AMBULANCE AT COLLEGE HORTICULTURALE RUE DU COLLEGE

ESTAIRES

TABLE I.

	Morning of 10.5.15 to 9 p.m. 10.5.15								9 p.m. 10.5.15 to 9 p.m. 11.5.15								9 p.m. 11.5.15 to 9 p.m. 12.5.15								9 p.m. 12.5.15 to 9 p.m. 13.5.15								9 p.m. 13.5.15 to 9 p.m. 14.5.15							
	GUNSHOT WOUNDS				SHELL WOUNDS				BAYONET WOUNDS				GUNSHOT WOUNDS				SHELL WOUNDS				BAYONET WOUNDS				GUNSHOT WOUNDS				SHELL WOUNDS				BAYONET WOUNDS				SHELL WOUNDS				BAYONET WOUNDS			
	Officers	Other Ranks	Indians	Germans	Officers	Other Ranks	Indians	Germans	Officers	Other Ranks	Indians	Germans	Officers	Other Ranks	Indians	Germans	Officers	Other Ranks	Indians	Germans	Officers	Other Ranks	Indians	Germans	Officers	Other Ranks	Indians	Germans	Officers	Other Ranks	Indians	Germans	Officers	Other Ranks	Indians	Germans	Officers	Other Ranks	Indians	Germans	Officers	Other Ranks	Indians	Germans
	4	74	—	1	1	37	—	—	1	11	—	—	5	36	1	—	—	15	—	—	1	—	—	—	6	86	3	1	3	140	3	—	—	3	1	—	8	155	53	1	1	6	144	5	1	—	6	—	—	—	38	1	—	1	37	—	—	1	1	—	—

TABLE II.

PERIODS	GUNSHOT WOUNDS					SHELL WOUNDS					BAYONET WOUNDS					TOTAL WOUNDED
	Officers	Other Ranks	Indians	Germans	Total	Officers	Other Ranks	Indians	Germans	Total	Officers	Other Ranks	Indians	Germans	Total	
Morning 10.5.15 to 9 p.m. 10.5.15	4	74	—	—	78	1	37	1	—	39	1	11	—	—	12	119
9 p.m. 10.5.15 to 9 p.m. 11.5.15	5	36	1	1	43	—	13	—	—	13	—	—	—	—	—	56
9 p.m. 11.5.15 to 9 p.m. 12.5.15	9	156	10	5	180	2	140	3	4	149	1	—	3	—	4	333
9 p.m. 12.5.15 to 9 p.m. 13.5.15	8	155	23	1	187	6	144	5	2	157	—	5	—	—	5	346
9 p.m. 13.5.15 to 9 p.m. 14.5.15	1	36	—	—	37	1	58	—	—	59	—	1	—	—	1	97
TOTALS	27	457	33	7	534	10	380	8	7	#14	1	11	1	—	13	951

3/15
16/15

Note. Tables include wounded from J.G. and Indian Divisions

E L Stanfo
Lieut Colonel R.A.M.C.
O/C No. 21 Field Ambulance

121/5256

Summarised.

21st Field Amb balance

Vol IV

WAR DIARY
INTELLIGENCE SUMMARY
(Erase heading not required.)

Army Form C. 2118.

Hour, Date, Place	Summary of Events and Information	Remarks and references to Appendices
1915.		
1st April ESTAIRES.	Enemy drops bomb from aeroplane on ESTAIRES	
2 do.	Received from G.H.Q 4 motor ambulance motor waggons & 1 Repair 2°	
	(4 Ford & 1 Sunbeam)	
5.90— do.	These cars went withdrawn to G.H.Q for work elsewhere.	
13 do. do.	Lt Mann relieves Lt Freeman Senr in temp' m/charge of 22nd Brigade	
	Lt A Suttie who retains duty gone from 7 Div'n Reserves proceed in relief	
14 do do	of Lt Miller M.O. 2nd W.R. placed on sick list	
	Lt Jardine to O'Reilly with 36 men proceed to form advanced Dressing	
	Station for wounded relief of 2nd & 3rd Bde R.A. who go into trenches	
15.90— do	around dusk. 4 some 7 Div' men & 5 Cav' who passed Day	
	on 7 Days leave to England.	
	Lt Col B. HORROCKS Rame (Empty) James from 23rd F.Amb.ce over to Cassel	
17.90— do	to permanent mess charge of 2/n Wks	
	Capt. H RANGAT left for No 10 General Clearing Station & furlough	
19. do do	with Capt H ETGMENT Rame who arrived to day — South end of	
	most reconnaisance of certain houses taken at South end of	
	SAILLY — FROMELLES Road & Rue Bacquerot as advanced Dressing	
	Station in care of activity occurring was accompanied by Dr.Dm.7 Div'n	
	& O.C. 22nd & 23rd F.A.	
20 do do	Lt E McKenzie Rame (temp) from temp' duty in 25th B.F.A.'s	
21 90— do	Lt E Glinton returns from temp' duty in 28th B.F.A.'s	
22 90— do	Lt Clinton replaces Lt Suttie with 2 W.R.C. for 7 days	
	& proceed to England on 8 days leave — started men along V 21 F.S. &	
	Majr hd. O'KELLY Rame — started men under orders G.H.Q as A.D.M.S	
23.90— do	Major Kelly proceeds to Boulogne	
	Capt ETGMENT left to command V 21st F.A.	E.G.A.

Army Form C. 2118.

WAR DIARY
or
INTELLIGENCE SUMMARY
(Erase heading not required.)

Instructions regarding War Diaries and Intelligence Summaries are contained in F. S. Regs., Part II. and the Staff Manual respectively. Title pages will be prepared in manuscript.

Hour, Date, Place	Summary of Events and Information	Remarks and references to Appendices
1915.		
24 April ESTAIRES	About 7 Dr inspected Ambulance Billets + three lines - at 6 pm received following message from same "O.W. "all sick of your unit "Should be immediately evacuated to No 23 F.A. You should send B.2 round "2 horse waken" inspected by G.O.C. 2nd Div. who stated that we were unlikely to move but must be ready to do so at 2 hours notice.	
25 do do		
26 do do	Opened "A" Section + recommenced receiving casualties of 21st Bde	
27 do do	Instructed by 2 and Div. 5 army for Lt. O'Balk to visit 24 F.A's at G.H.Q with regard to his application for a permanent commission in Army. Major Hope ECD Hayes Roan relieved ——— Command of 22 F.A.	
28 do do (11.30am)	Orders to move to STRAZEELE - arrive there 4.30 pm tomorrow Station - Lt. Howards rejoined -	
29 do do	Saw S.O.C. 27th Inf. A.D. at 9am - No orders yet	
30 do do	Nil -	

E C Hayes Helman
OC 21st F.A.mbce

amd.

Summarised 121/5506

1st Division

21st Field Ambulance

Vol II

121/6506

May 1915

51

WAR DIARY

INTELLIGENCE SUMMARY

Army Form C. 2118.

Hour, Date, Place	Summary of Events and Information	Remarks and references to Appendices
1915. 2nd May STAZEELE.	Rev: G.H. COLBECK C. of E. Chaplain attached for 7 days leave.	
3 do	Lt. M.J. Johnston R.A.M.C. (Temp.) joined from No. 16 Sanitary Section.	
4 do	Rev. G.F. TRENCH C. of E. Chaplain joined vice Rev. Colbeck (from No.10 Cas. Clearing). Marched to ESTAIRES at 8 p.m. via MERRIS + BLEU. Billeted in our old billets & buildings of College Horticultural. Arrived midnight.	
5 do ESTAIRES.	Opened "A" Tent Sub Dist. Here & "C" Bearer with 2 officers & Town Ambulance. Adv. Dressing Station at LE DRUMEZ (Map M.2.8.) as before. 13th 21st Inf. Bde camped FAUQUISSAT ("F Line of Trenches.")	Sheet 36 Belgium 1:40000
6 do	Opened "B" Tent in addition to "A". To prepare for a proposed attack in conjunction with the 8th Div on FROMELLES + AUBERS. Made reconnaissance with A.D.M.S. & O.C. 2a, 22, 23 F.A. of proposed advanced Dressing Stations at Rue de Bout. & certain dug-outs.	
9th do	First day of attack. 2/3rd Bearer Div lifted 6.30 a.m. for G.34.13. "C" Bearer landing at M.2.13. Map Sheet 36 Belgium 1:40000 — 8th Dist. only engaged. 4 of our casualties from 7 Div. 1.30 from 8th Div dealt with. Messages of transactions annexed. Appendix I.	Appendix I annexed.
10th do	2nd day of attack — Total Casualties Received 31— 23 of R.E. & 8 I.7 Div. Ordered by A.D.M.S. to close & march to BETHUNE. 2.16 p.m. Reached BETHUNE at 12.20 midnight.	
11th do BETHUNE	Reconnaissance with A.D.M.S. & Dir. of Adv. Posts at X.18.8 (Rifle BETHUNE Trench) Sheet 1 10000. Estaminet Adv. Dressing Station for 2.12.8.p.p.H. in Trenches. Leaves for our. Also saw Adv Post. X.17.13 & R.24.a BETHUNE at 6 p.m. Opened "A" Tent Sub Div at L'ECOLE MATERNELLE. Saw D.G.O. 2 informed keeping Bearer Div 1/3 to 1/2 C. in reserve at Military Ground. LA QUIN QU'RUE. Adv. Bhors in connection with proposed attack on LA QUIN QU'RUE.	

Army Form C. 2118.

WAR DIARY
or
INTELLIGENCE SUMMARY
(Erase heading not required.)

Hour, Date, Place	Summary of Events and Information	Remarks and references to Appendices
1915		
12th May. BETHUNE	Received orders from Cav:Bde to march to ESSARS & open an Adv. ("B") Left at 3pm opened at 4pm at Ecole maire. Convoy arrived at 5pm. Vacated the Station 15 Evacuated Sick & the Sick & Dis. Lt.FINCKIBBIN RAMC(S.R.) joined. Vice Lt Luck wounded at the 10th at SAILLY-PROMENCHES & at 25?	
13 May – ESSARS	Lt. BAIRD RAMC(T) joined from N°4 Gen Hosp. VERSAILLES	
14 do	Orders for attack postponed. Ret. home.	
	Met a Bn 70th wounded Cav. Pats. & two locals ?? at ??n Ambulance happen Parlaymen – Visited G.O.C. 70th at Cam. du Point –	
16 do	To absorb a large number of Terr.s of 2/1 HINGES by A.D.M.S. Lt Col. Ruffell	
	a 2 men in charge	
	Lt Baird & officer Temp.in.Command to N°2 F.A. at BETHUNE then San ???	
	Lt Johnston do	
	Full particulars of operations in attack on La Quinque Rue set out in annexes appendix N°2	appendix N°2 attached
17 9o	adm.s 70th & relieve L. Johnston. To meet Chance of 2.Reg.Sikh. Evac. me 4	
	Guncha Rame wounded.	
	To adv Dressing Station WIK ams 70 in	
18 9o	4 Shells near ESS H.Q.S. Rue LEPINETTE & Dressing Station.	
	Invalids adv Dressing Station	
19 9o	Capt? Gaunt RAMC? all wounded cleared. Ordered him ?? ambulance Station Personnel & equipt to return to H.Qs at ESSARS. Lt O'Reilly with "C" Section Bearer & Evac.in went relieved by Canadian Lt. Gordon to command at adv.Dressing Station till then- arranged for 1 H?	
	Ambulance N°7 & Lt. FLEMING Ramc joined- ambulance on Est 13th & 21st & 8 on 13th. withdrawn	
	Marched Complete Ambulance & 2 horse waggons with R.A. to ROBECQ allotted Billets for Cav.Bde Hospital in Brasserie Avis.	
	ROBECQ	EN

Army Form C. 2118.

WAR DIARY
or
INTELLIGENCE SUMMARY

(Erase heading not required.)

Instructions regarding War Diaries and Intelligence Summaries are contained in F.S. Regs., Part II. and the Staff Manual respectively. Title pages will be prepared in manuscript.

Hour, Date, Place	Summary of Events and Information	Remarks and references to Appendices
1915. ROBECQ.	SOMS 1st Corps kroms 7 O.R. visited me.	
20 May	Lt-Gen FLEMING Rmc(T) - To meet enquiry of effects of accdt Beirol -	
21 do	Lt. 7E Anjot Rmc(T) joined -	
22 do	Visited 600 21st Bpo 81st - Inspected Bde Ambulance	
23 do	Bathing Parades of whole Battalion - Males Egand J O.R.	
24 do	Lt. S. Man to 7 days leave	
27 do	To report by Gen. Joffre to 7 E Dwn	
30 do	Lt. Jacobus Remc a 7 days leave to England.	
31 do	Lt. Man rejoined	

E. Flags
Lt. O.C. Rmc.
OC 21st 1st Anthelm

Appendix I

21st F.A.

Ref's map
Sheet 36 Belgium
in 40,000

Report on the Medical Transactions of the 21st Field Ambulance during the active period 9th + 10th May 1915.

Having had previous conferences with the ADMS 7 Divn as to general dispositions of the attack on the FROMELLES – AUBERS area by the 8th & 7th Divn & also in Company with him, his DADMS & the OC's 22nd & 23rd Field Amb ces having made reconnaissance of the ground it was decided to establish in the first phase of the action a Divl. Collecting Station & advanced Dressing Stations at the ROUGE de BOUT (M.36.d. map) These premises were to be occupied by the 22nd + 23rd Ambulances whose affiliated Brigades were to come into action before that of the Bde to which the 21st F.A. is affiliated ie the 21st Infy Bde.

The latter Brigade were in reserve for the most part but also held "F" line of trenches ie from PICANTIN to FAUQUISART. (Map M.12d to N.7.d)

The already existing advanced dressing Station of the 21st Field Ambulance at Le DRUMEZ (map M.29.a) with "C" Sec Bearer Sub Divn under Lt O'REILLY Ramc was detailed to afford medical relief for "F" line – It cleared casualties from the Regtl aid Posts on the Rue Bacquerot more particularly from that of the 4th Camerons at M.13.c. This was done by 2 motor Ambulance Waggons from Le DRUMES at 9 pm to 9 am each day.

On the first day of the attack A+B Sect Bearer Sub Divns marched to Farm at G.34.b just N of the Railway an intercommunication Cyclist orderly going ahead to the advanced Dressy Station of the 22nd Field Ambulance at ROUGE de BOUT So that when the 22nd advanced the 21 F.A. was to occupy in the 2nd phase of the attack the premises & subsequently proceed to dug outs behind the 21st Infy Bde at H.31.c.

1915
9th May

1915

10th May

As the 21st & 22nd F.B. main body did not come into action & the [illegible] Brigades did not advance but remained at [illegible] the night of the 9th/10th. On the morning of the 10th however, B section of 2 Div Bearers under Lt. Col. Linton Rance proceeded to the Rue Petillon in order of [illegible] & assisted the 5th Div in collecting wounded. They did. They removed 40 to 60 cases from the trench [illegible] in fours — Unfortunately during these operations Lt. Col. Linton Rance was wounded (Bullet wound of left thigh) — Lt. Stanrooke succeeded him in command.

At 12 noon I received orders from A.D.M.S. of Div to [illegible] & be prepared to march with the Div to another place —

All sick & casualties who had been brought to the main dressing station of the 21st Field Ambulance at [illegible] and [illegible] at Turkmee and Estaires were sent to the 1st & 3rd Lahore Field Ambulance at Estaires — & the 21st Field Amb. held speedy & ready to march — The adv. dressing station at Le Drumez closed & the bearers of C [illegible] joined Head Quarters at 4.20 p.m. — At 5.30 the A & B sections came back. Div. also rejoined — orders were received from the A.D.M.S. at 6 p.m. to march at 8 p.m. to Bethune, where the Ambulance arrived without incident at 12 midnight —

I append a Table showing the casualties & sick received by the 2nd F.A. during this period — they were nearly all from the 5th Div — & only amounted in all to 31 —

E.L. Haydon
Lt. Col. R.A.M.C.
O.C. 2nd F.A.

16 May 1915

Appendix II

Reference Map
Sheet 36c. 13
BÉTHUNE
= (1/40000)

Report on the Medical arrangements of the 21st Field Ambulance during the period of activity near La Quinque Rue from 16th May to 19th May inclusive.

May 16.

The 2nd & 20th Bde attacked at 3.15 a.m. The 21st Bde. to which the 21st Field Ambulance is affiliated remained in reserve trenches & dugouts in the Rue l'Épinette (X.18 & 24 map.). The Bearer Sub Divs. of the 21st F.A. were available & did assist those of the 22nd & 23rd F.A. in the collection of casualties in the first phase & subsequently collected the casualties of the 21st Inf. Bde. when the latter came into action. but during the whole period of activity the 2 Tent Sub Divisions of the 21st F.A. (A & C) were parked at ESSARS. "B" Section however opened at that place in the École & Mairie (map X.25 a) & received the whole of the sick of the 7th Division — (A table is appended shewing the numbers of sick so there treated.)

Two advanced dressing stations were opened on the 16/5/15, one at S.W. B. Rue du Bois for 20th Bde & one at X.24 a in the Rue l'Épinette for the 22nd Bde. It was from the latter the Bearer Sub Div. of the 21st F.A. operated as a point d'appui until 21.F.A. actually took over the Advanced Dressing Station.

A Divisional Collecting Station was formed by the 21st F.A. at Le TOURET (map X.16 b.d.) where walking cases received attention & lorries readjusted & light to park. Here also an officer & N.C.O of the 21st F.A. regulated the supply & route of the pooled Motor Ambulance Waggons of 21st, 22nd & 23rd F.A. augmented by those of the 47th London Div. making a total of 22 Motor Ambulance Waggons & helped also by the spare horsed ambulance waggons of the Ambulances of the 7th Div. All wounded were sent from here to Field Ambulances Tent Sub Divs at BÉTHUNE. (22nd, 23rd, 5 & 6 London F.As).

Two Horsed Ambulance Waggons were attached the R.A. i.e 1 to 22nd Bde R.F.A & 1 to 14 Bde R.H.A) for assistance to those units in action.

At night time this date 'A' & 'B' Sub Divs 21 F.A. helped in collection of 20th & 22nd Bde Casualties.

17 May
"B" Sub Div Bearers were sent up to Le TOURET in the first place subsequently to Adv. Dressing Station at Rue l'Épinette which was taken over by the 21st F.A.

17th May (cont'd)
the 21st Inf.Bd. F.A. having gone into action that morning. The 22nd F.A. Bearer Sub.Divn. also assisted the 21st Bearers during this day & night in collection of casualties.

18th May
The same process of collection proceeded but the 22nd F.A. Bearers were withdrawn to Le TOURET, on much needed rest & the A.D.M.S. 7 Divn. sent up Bearers of 4th London Field Amb.Ce., to assist. This was much appreciated by the tired Bearers of 21st F.A.

19th May
The 4 London Divn. F.A. Bearers not being required as by this time the attack had ceased & all casualties having been recovered & wounded removed, were withdrawn. Troops of the Canadian Divisn. gradually relieved the 21st Inf.Bde. & the Canadian F.A. Bearers took over & relieved 21st F.A. of the Advanced Dressing Station at X.24.a. The A.D.M.S. 7 Divn. gave orders to me to withdraw the 21st F.A. & march to ROBECQ. & billet there with the 21st Inf.Bde. This was successfully done. One casualty however occurred amongst the horses. "L.E.-anette" that was heavily shelled at times.

I append a list of names of officers & men of the 21st F.A. who during this period performed excellent work.

E.C. Hayes
Lt Col R.A.M.C.
O.C. 21st F.A.

21. May 1915.
ROBECQ.

STATEMENT OF CASES ADMITTED TO 21st FIELD AMBULANCE

PERIOD 16½s – 20½s

SICK

7' DIVISION

UNIT	SICK
Grenadier Guards	3
Scots Guards	1
Border Regiment	6
Gordon Highlanders	2
2nd R.S.	4
Wilts R.	2
Bedford R.	7
R. Warwick R.	1
Queens	2
Staffs	3
1st Wilts R.A.M.C.	2
Cameronians	1
Gordon Highlanders	2
Royal Scots	4
Cyclist Coy. 7 Divn.	3
A Co A.S.C. (7 Div Train)	2
5th Co R.E.	1
22 Field Ambulance (nursing)	3
104 Fd R.F.C.	1
58 Fd R.F.A.	2
French Army (attch 4 Corps)	1
TOTAL	**57**

OTHER IMPERIAL DIV.

	SICK
1 Rensington R. (Pershans)	1
4 H.S.R.	2
1 Wilts R.	3
8 King's Liverpool R.	1
R.T.R. S/58	—
R.E. 3rd T.A.B.	—
R.G.A. 06th Hy.	—
TOTAL	**10**

OTHER DIVISIONS

	Cases Admitted
Indian Cav. Div.	3
Cand 10D Divs.R	15
Indian (details)	2
TOTAL	**20**

TOTAL

7 Division	57
Other Imperial Divisions	10
Other Divisions	20
TOTAL	**74**

Remit to Zaorida Dorsac. he cures twaring orders.
— No others admit during 24hrs period.

E. Hayls
Capt.

Capt. Lieut Colonel O Banks
Lieut Ambulance

No. 21st FIELD AMBULANCE

RETURN SHOWING WOUNDED ADMITTED AND EVACUATED DURING THE OPERATIONS

0/9/10 [illegible] 06
2 July

DIVISIONS	INFANTRY, MACHINE GUN CORPS & R.F.C.						INFANTRY, O.M.C., R.F.C. & C.S.					TOTAL	REMARKS
	RIFLE WOUNDS		ARTILLERY WOUNDS		BAYONET WOUNDS		RIFLE WOUNDS		ARTILLERY WOUNDS	GAS & OTHER	DAYS NOT INCL		
	Officers	Other Ranks	Officers	Other Ranks	Officers	Other Ranks	Officers	Other Ranks	Officers	Other Ranks		Officers	Other Ranks
VII Division		1	1	1				1		1			8
VIII Division		6		3		1		1	1	4	1		25
Other Divisions													
Indians													
Germans													
TOTALS	0	0	1	4	1	1		1	1			0	51

Summarized

10/5993

12/5993

4th Division

21st Field Ambulance

Vol VI

June 1918

18

auto

WAR DIARY
INTELLIGENCE SUMMARY

Army Form C. 2118.

Hour, Date, Place	Summary of Events and Information	Remarks and references to Appendices
1915		
3 June – ROBECQ	Lt Baird to DADOS for supervision of knock helmets & anti Gas. Ordered by ADMS 7 Divn to hand over tentage & ambulance to field Ambulance – Lt Sinnan to 23 F.A. to help during attack.	
4 " do –	3 operation tents handed over to No 23 F.A.	
5 " do	Reconnoitred AVELETTE under orders of ADMS. 7 Divn. Borrowed 12 native Jalls Indian Tents from No 1 Broucks Clearing Station by orders of Divn 1st Army. arranged to	
6 " do	Reconnaissance with ADMS 7 Divn. & OC 22 FA for site for Camp for Ambulances.	
	Lt O'Reilly made reconnaissance towards GIVENCHY for an Adv. Dressing Station. – All my motor cars reported to OC 23 FA @ 7 P.M. for duty in clearing wounded from a proposed attack	
7 " do	Lt Jardine returns from leave. Deld. Efford –	
8 " do	Lt Sinnan rejoined from leave. – visited Avelette	
	Drew No 12 Indian Tents – visited Avelette	
9 " do	Received 2 Ford Cars with Drivers	
10 " AVELETTE	"A" Section Bearer Sub Dvn to AVELETTE at 8.15 a.m. — whole of Field Ambulance marched 4 pm. arrived 8.30 p.m. at AVELETTE. ADMS 4th Corps inspected camp. also GOC 4th Corps. Made reconnaissance with ADMS 7 Divn. Thursday, Evening Chief & the Tuning Fort. Met Lt Jardine to O'Reilly have seen GOC 21 & 22 FA etc. Sand bagging & OTs at Tuning Corner –	

EAW

Army Form C. 2118.

WAR DIARY
or
INTELLIGENCE SUMMARY
(Erase heading not required.)

Hour, Date, Place	Summary of Events and Information	Remarks and references to Appendices
1915		
12 June ABLETTE	Conference with Regimental half officers of 21st MB & Sen. Medical officers & Major Gaunt.	
13 do	Proposed by G.Medn. March 1 Cavalry Bugon. To superintend the Gas Chamber — Inspected by Corps Staffs — Sent workingparty to Trundy Corner —	
14 do	Received general orders of admn. 70th — Landing of ammd. with DC 22 FA for 3 Brit Machine Ration Carriers to be sent to a station at GORRE. Attacked enemy near GIVENCHY.	See appendix No 1 arranged as to gunners Total of wounded last WK
15 do		
16 Do 10.30pm Do	Lt T.E. ArryOT Came to M.O i/c 2 Bed pts vice Lt Fleming killed — "A" Lcl's Beamis returned — 18 HC. DTS B'Murphy — handed over to DSS	
17 Do	& Carrier to No 2 FA at Windy Corner	
18 do	Rev Trench reprind Offick Mess	
19 do	Capt E.T. GAUNT Came to England on 7 days leave —	
20 do	Lt-Dr Mann to Murphy had Charge + (Cremino)	
21 do	Lt A.T. MacCrosky Came on Duty from 24th FA —	
23 do	Rain. Med Board on Sgt Shaw + Bedford for a Commission —	
24 do	Wet	
25 do	Heavy Rain	
26 do	Fine — Camp drying up —	
27 do	Capt N Gaunt returned — Lcl's Beamis to LE TOURET ind Klahm	
30th do	Lt O'Reilly + 2 min to leave to England & "A" Bearers 13 Beamis 73 PC for 1st Fd Dm marked to HAM EN ARTOIS	CE Mays LMCC Cdn OC 21st FA

Appendix I

Reference map 1 in 40,000
BETHUNE
Sheet 36c 1b

Report of the medical arrangements of the 21st Field Ambulance during the period of activity near GIVENCHY from 6 pm 15th to 9 am the 19th June 1915.

=

10th June 1915. The Main Dressing Station of the 21st F.A. was established in Tents including 12 Native Indian pattern borrowed from No. 1 Casualty Clearing Station. It was situated at AVELETTES (W.17.a). It had accommodation for nearly 300 patients.

Short general particulars of a proposed attack near Givenchy by the 21st Infantry Bde having been received I proceeded with the ADMS & DADMS 7 Divn & 2 of my Bearer Officers to make a reconnaissance to confirm the selection of an Advanced Dressing Station which the latter officers had made — i.e. a House at A.7.d at "Windy Corner" & certain Dug Outs at "WESTMINSTER BRIDGE" (map F.13.a) as an overflow. These positions were approved.

12th June Held a conference with my Bearer Officers & O.Co of Battns of 21st Infy Bde explaining arrangements.

13th do Sent a working party of Bearers to Adv. Dressing Station at W.7.d to place Sandbags & work under R.E. in making dug outs.

14 do Received RAMC Operation Orders from ADMS 7th Divn.

15 do. Issued my own in conformity therewith which involved
(1) Sending to Adv. Dressing Station at "Windy CORNER". "C" Sectn Bearer Sub Divn under Lt. O'Reilly with water cart & Forage cart.
(2) "A" & "B" Sectn Bearer Sub Divns with "B" Forage cart with extra Blankets, dressings, medical comforts & extra Stretchers to "Westminster Bridge" — 3 Brooke Mac Cormac Stretcher Carriers were taken to "Windy Corner" & subsequently 2 Ashford litters taken into use, which were of great help to the Bearers between Adv. Dressing Stn & "Westminster Bridge" Dug Outs.

The whole Adv. Dressing Station were placed under the command of Capt. E.T. GAUNT.

The ADMS 7 Divn parked the Motor Ambulances & 3 Horsed waggons at CHATEAU GORRE to ply between the Adv. D. Stn & Dug outs & the Main Dressing Station at AVELETTES.

The attack opened at 6 pm. but previous to this the 21st Infy Bde who were in reserve Dug Outs near "Windy Corner" had a few casualties which were received here before that hour. During the night of the 15th/16th from 6 pm. 15th to 9 am 16th roughly 250 Casualties were received at Main Dressing Station, this however included 70 cases of so called Shell Shock & cases who had been buried by the trenches falling in. The majority of which were kept only for the night & discharged to attend their Regtl medl Inspectn Rooms the following morning.

16th June 15. For the period from 9 am 16th to 9 am 17th the number of casualties dealt with were 234, which includes similarly cases of "Shell Shock" to the number of 24 + which were of a mild nature.

On the evening of the 16th about 6 pm the neighbourhood of the Adv. Dressing Station was so heavily shelled that Capt. Gaunt withdrew all the personnel to the dug outs at Westminster Bridge (Lt O'Reilly & 4 Bearers only remaining in Dug Outs at W.7.a). The Dressing Station however was reoccupied next Day.

17 June 1915 — During the period 9 am 17th to 9 am 18th there were 29 wound casualties, not including a few "Shell Shocks".

The 21st Infy Bde were withdrawn from action their place being taken by the 22nd Infantry Bde. On the evening of this day the Adv Dressing Station at "Windy Corner" (A.7.0) & the Dug outs at "Westminster Bridge" were vacated by the 3 Bearer Sub Divns of the 21st Field Ambulance — "B & C" returning to their previous Billets at W.30.3 & "A" to Hd Qrs at AVELETTES — No 22 F.A. took over the Adv Dressing Station & Dug outs.

18 June. From 9 am 18th to 9 am 19th there were only 6 wound casualties, not including 2 "Shell Shocks".

During the whole period under review there was only 1 Death in the 21st Field Ambulance but 3 bodies were received for burial from No 2 Ambulance Flotilla.

I append a Table shewing in detail the numbers, nature of wounds & periods during which they occurred —

E C Hayes
Lt Col RAMC
OC 21st F.A.

19th June 1915.

TABLES SHEWING WOUNDED ADMITTED TO AND EVACUATED FROM MAIN DRESSING STATION.

No. 21 FIELD AMBULANCE

Vinglette

TABLE I.

	From 6 p.m. 15-6-15 to 9 a.m. 16-6-15									From 9 a.m. 16-6-15 to 9 a.m. 17-6-15									From 9 a.m. 17-6-15 to 9 a.m. 18-6-15									From 9 a.m. 18-6-15 to 9 p.m. 19-6-15								
	GUNSHOT WOUNDS			SHELL WOUNDS			BAYONET WOUNDS			GUNSHOT WOUNDS			SHELL WOUNDS			BAYONET WOUNDS			GUNSHOT WOUNDS			SHELL WOUNDS			BAYONET WOUNDS			GUNSHOT WOUNDS			SHELL WOUNDS			BAYONET WOUNDS		
	Officers	Other Ranks	Germans	Officers	Other Ranks	Germans	Officers	Other Ranks	Germans	Officers	Other Ranks	Germans	Officers	Other Ranks	Germans	Officers	Other Ranks	Germans	Officers	Other Ranks	Germans	Officers	Other Ranks	Germans	Officers	Other Ranks	Germans	Officers	Other Ranks	Germans	Officers	Other Ranks	Germans	Officers	Other Ranks	Germans
	1*	38		9	9†214			3			66		4	164	1		2	1		11			18						2			4				

† French Army. * Bomb wounds.

TABLE II.

PERIOD	GUNSHOT WOUNDS				SHELL WOUNDS				BAYONET WOUNDS				TOTAL	REMARKS
	Officers	Other Ranks	Germans	Total	Officers	Other Ranks	Germans	Total	Officers	Other Ranks	Germans	Total		
6pm15-6-15 to 9am16-6-15		39		39	9	214		223		3		3	265	9 French Army
9am16/6 to 9am17/6		66		66	4	165	1	170		2		2	238	† 13 bomb wounds
9am17/6 to 9am18/6		11		11		18		18					29	
9am18/6 to 9am19/6		2		2		4		4					6	
Total		118		118	13	401 †	1	415		5		5	538	

E. Stamp
Lieut Col. Comdg.
Comdg 21st Fd. Amb.

28/9/15

121/6341

Ans

7th B Battalion

121/6341

21st Field Ambulance

Vol VIII

July 16.

Army Form C. 2118

WAR DIARY
—or—
INTELLIGENCE SUMMARY
(Erase heading not required.)

Instructions regarding War Diaries and Intelligence Summaries are contained in F.S. Regs., Part II. and the Staff Manual respectively. Title Pages will be prepared in manuscript.

Place	Date	Hour	Summary of Events and Information	Remarks and references to Appendices
HAM EN ARTOIS	1915 1st May		The whole of the 21st Field Ambulance reaches this place at 2 pm.	
do	4 „		Lt O'Reilly's leave expended 4 days by the W.O.	
do	5 „		Lt Saint to temporary duty charge of 3/7 13th RFA	
do	6 „		Lt A Chilli [?] duty back to No 14 General Clearing Station suffering from colitis.	
do	7 „		Lt Stafford to temporary duty charge 35/13th RFA	
do	9 „		Lt McLoughey received from RSM? acting as Sgt Maj during absence of Col Stan to 7 days leave to England	
do	10 „		21st & 7th & 10th Field Trenches Jn of La Clinique Rue	
do	11 „		"A" Sec Bearers marches to LE CORNER MALO (map Q 28. Sheet 28.3 Helfin 1:2000) thence to Kings Road Rue CHEVATTES (X.11.D) taking over Dressing Station from the present Div Ambulance there.	
ZELOBES	12 „		21st Field Ambulance (less A Bearers) marches to ZELOBES, via LE CORNER MALO Peppermts march over present road in form R.2.7 @ from 19 Biker at 8.30 am arriving 1.30 pm took over previous road (command of) Peppermts recruit Duty commencing under (command of).	
do	13 „		Advanced Dressing Stn Shields (1 front severely injured).	
do	15 „		Lt McGonaghey to tempy had charge Morte in relief of Lt Saint to leave.	
do	17 „		During tempy inspect	
do	18 „		Lt McGillow leave to England. Capt ParrinE Kadstator to see list of observations on mens [?] feet [?] pain [?] heaters beyond Hou — 21st Fa numbers sick	
do	19 „		Lt Jardine [?] McKibbon with A Sec on bearers reporting.	
do	23 „		Promoted 03.20 F.7 P. 7.8 white hat the lime Trenches taken as Tent & 3 Mc Tents for reception stations by orders of assist Dir Medic garrison. Contre anny of 2 Roope ration on. Recruit hospice Contre anny of 2 Roope ration on. Recruit holder Contre anny of 2 Roope ration on. Recruit holder Contre anny of 2 Roope ration on. Recruit water 40 21st Fa	
			Col Wallace Consulting bryd to face wateson	

E.E.H

P.T.O

Army Form C. 2118

WAR DIARY
or
INTELLIGENCE SUMMARY
(Erase heading not required.)

Instructions regarding War Diaries and Intelligence Summaries are contained in F.S. Regs., Part II. and the Staff Manual respectively. Title Pages will be prepared in manuscript.

Place	Date 1915	Hour	Summary of Events and Information	Remarks and references to Appendices
ZESLOBES	July 22	—	"B" Section Bearers under Lt. O'Reilly & Lt. McKibbin formed Advanced Dressing Station at St. MAAST POST (M.32.B) in dug outs for most ads of 7. 21st amp 8th who take out trench line 52 of LEBASSEE Road night of 22/23rd. Lt. Brockenham (2nd) the 7 days leave to England — St. omer nets. Lt. I.D Evans joined Regiment for duty. To adv Dressing Station at St. MAAST. Lt. D Evans proceed to permanent charge of 2/R.9 F. amb.	
do	" 23	—		
do	" 24	—		
do	" 26	—		
do	" 31	—	Lt. Col Sir Ian Leishman + Col B.S. Hemingham visit the Ambulance.	

E.A.Maybo
F. Le Quesne
O.C. 21st F.57th N.Div

6607/121

7th Division

21st Field Ambulance

Vol VIII

from 1 - 31. 8. 15

Aug '15

Army Form C. 2118

WAR DIARY
or
INTELLIGENCE SUMMARY
(Erase heading not required.)

Place	Date	Hour	Summary of Events and Information	Remarks and references to Appendices
LANNOY	1.8.15		2nd F.A. to LANNOY in Forts (near GONNEHEM)	
	3.		D.D.M.S. 1st Corps inspected F.A.	
			Sm reconnaissance with motor-ambulance received 5 made a reconnaissance of GONNEHEM with a view to obtaining winter quarters	
			Lieut. WOOD (S.R.) attached for instruction finding transport to 4th CAMERONS but STAFFORD to temporary md. charge of 4th CAMERONS.	
	4.		G.O.C. 7th Divson inspected the Ambulance.	
			S/Sgt. Major HALFORD proceeded on leave	
			Lieut. McKIBBON to Dr. TRENCH C.P. proceeded on leave	
	5.		Lieut. WOOD proceeded to Medical charge of 4th CAMERONS	
	9.		Lieut. McCONACHY proceeded to No. 2. C.C.M. hospital for duty	
			Pvt. B.E. WRIGHT joined for duty	
	12.		Lieut. McKIBBON & Sgt. Maj. HOLFORD returned from leave	

WAR DIARY or INTELLIGENCE SUMMARY

(Erase heading not required.)

Army Form C. 2118

Place	Date	Hour	Summary of Events and Information	Remarks and references to Appendices
LONNOY	15.8.15		Visited 22nd F.A.	
	16.8.15		New quotation completed. Visited A.D.M.S. at BUSNES and G.O.C. 2n'd Div. Lieut. O'REILLY placed on sick list with injury to knee.	
LA PUGY FERME	18		21st F.A. moved to LA PUGY FERME W.16.c. A.D.V. Dressing Station at F.G.A.C.	
	20.		Visited adv. dressing Station.	
			Lieut. O'REILLY evacuated to No.6.C.C.S. Lieut. T.S. STAFFORD proceeded to England on inspiration of contract. A.D.M.S. hospitals on advance.	
	21.		Lieut. FORD joined for duty.	
	25.		Lt. Colonel HAYES who had been for some days suffering from P.U.U.O was to-day evacuated to No.6 C.C.S. I accordingly took charge of the ambulance.	St Saint Capt. Dame C.
	26.		Lt. HURST from No.3. General Hospital joined for duty. Posted to A Sect Tontouta.	

2 F

Army Form C. 2118

WAR DIARY
or
INTELLIGENCE SUMMARY
(Erase heading not required.)

Place	Date	Hour	Summary of Events and Information	Remarks and references to Appendices
LA PLOU FERME	26.8.15		Received operation orders O/C of Bgde K stating that 21st Bgde will be relieved in trenches to-night by 20th Bgde; also that 4th Bgde taken over GIVENCHY section of line on night 26/27th from 5th Bgde.	
			Operation orders received from 7th Divisional HQrs stating 7th Division will be relieved by another Corps. 7th Division HQ to move about BUSNES. O/C of Bgde to be in [?] to 2nd Div. from 28th to 4 Sept inc. O/C F.A. to move to BERGUETTE 7 a.m. 28th.	
			Orders from A.D.M.S. to hand over ADS to 23rd FA. by 11 a.m. on 28th.	
			Arranged relief of ADS with OC 23rd FA	
			Visited A.D.S.	
			Sgt KENDLE rejoined at own request, evacuated to No 1 C.C.S. CHOCQUES	
	Qn A		Lieut MCKIBBON returned from ADS	
			Visited B + A D.M.G 7th Div & obtained billeting area. Visited billeting area at BERGUETTE 016.A. No suitable building for hospital as both are short accommodating a billeting area. 3/	

Army Form C. 2118

WAR DIARY
or
INTELLIGENCE SUMMARY
(Erase heading not required.)

Place	Date	Hour	Summary of Events and Information	Remarks and references to Appendices
LA PLOU FERME	27.8.15		Lt. WRIGHT assumed from Comp. and charge of 2nd BEDS REGT	
BERGUETTE	28.8.15		moved to BERGUETTE started at 7.15 a.m. arrived at 11.15 a.m. via ROBECQUE BUSNE and GUARBECQUE. Car moved by approximate convoy of 26 carts.	
	29th		Inoculated 2 corps (no horses + no Hammershaft) 22 c.c. at AIRE. Returned 6 cans to dust. (all by own cars) Forwarded programmes of proposed units to march to A.D.M.S. in accordance with instructions received.	
	30th		21st F.A. proceeded a route march.	

(T-S) appt
C/Lt O am C

4

7th Division

12/7053

Summarised

21st Field Ambulance

Vol IX

Sep 1. 15

Sep '15

Army Form C. 2118

WAR DIARY
or
INTELLIGENCE SUMMARY
(Erase heading not required.)

Instructions regarding War Diaries and Intelligence Summaries are contained in F. S. Regs., Part II. and the Staff Manual respectively. Title Pages will be prepared in manuscript.

Place	Date	Hour	Summary of Events and Information	Remarks and references to Appendices
BERGUETTE	1.9.15		A D M S visited ambulance. He sent the beds by motor ambulance until fit to continue.	
	2.9.15		Received instructions from A.D.M.S. - to move on 3rd & 23rd to GONNEHEM, train to move 6 p.m. to open there one section for treatment of sick of Division. Visited 21st Bde H.Qrs at Cerne and tried to try to get in touch in form dry's. 21st Bde Hdqrs returned to WATERLOO Bridge and obtained billeting area at GONNEHEM and fixed on School at V12 C 53. For Hospital and Farm at V12 C 22 for Details. Chief medical officer and my two orderly staff sergeants arrived at SCSE 12220.25. Lt JARDINE and one section proceeded to GONNEHEM as an advance party.	
	3.9.15		Starting at 9.30 A.M. Remainder of personnel left at 5 P.M. Arriving at GONNEHEM at 7.15 p.m. Received instructions from A.D.M.S. to send in two motor cars to report and escort my the till the 3rd one officer and 30 men to report at fortifying the A.D.S. at the CHATEAU VERMELLES tonight and escort old CHATEAU to arrive at 7.15 p.m. and there old Clayhook CAPT O'REILLY proceeded as above with 30 teams of one section	
GONNEHEM.	4.9.15		Received instructions from A.D.M.S. Ward from 10 A.M. today the 22nd + 23rd F.A's will lessen sick and wounded, evacuated to Div. 22nd or 23rd F.A. such to be brought up to 21st F.A and shown there as Divisional Admin train	

Army Form C. 2118

WAR DIARY
or
INTELLIGENCE SUMMARY
(Erase heading not required.)

Instructions regarding War Diaries and Intelligence Summaries are contained in F.S. Regs., Part II. and the Staff Manual respectively. Title Pages will be prepared in manuscript.

Place	Date	Hour	Summary of Events and Information	Remarks and references to Appendices
GONNEHEM	5.9.15		S.M. HOLFORD evacuated to No 9 CCS, LILLERS suffering from severe colitis. Arranged for him to be returned to the ambulance if possible.	
	6.9.15		S.M. COPELAND returned from leave. A.D.M.S visited the Ambulance. Received direct from Hants S hersel & forwarded to Divisin M.G. Workshops.	
	7.9.15		Took over Command of 21st F.A. from Capt E.T. GAUNT. W.T. Knight Lt. Col R.A.M.C	
	8.9.15		LT. J.T. HURST left today according to instructions received from A.D.M.S 6/9/15. Received instructions from A.D.M.S to collect the sick of the 20th Bgde Amm. Col. at 10am 7th. Division troops in the GONNEHEM area from the 8th inst., to collect all sick and send Channel out-20 probst him for strong church img Wehen at 10am Divl Troops A.D.S. VERMELLES. Sick and wounded of the 21st Bgde will be collected by the 23rd F.A. from the 9th inst. A.D.M.S visited the Ambulance. Received instructions from A.D.M.S to place at the disposal of the C.R.E. 7th Divn in the town both wing party to help in general fatigue wg. the A.D.S & hand 1 party to hd CHATEAU VERMELLES find working at 7.15 9/15 to relieve No Amb.wing	
	9.9.15			

Army Form C. 2118

WAR DIARY
or
INTELLIGENCE SUMMARY
(Erase heading not required.)

Instructions regarding War Diaries and Intelligence Summaries are contained in F.S. Regs., Part II. and the Staff Manual respectively. Title Pages will be prepared in manuscript.

Place	Date	Hour	Summary of Events and Information	Remarks and references to Appendices
GONNEHEM	10.9.15		I proceeded on leave this afternoon. Handed over command to CAPT E.T. GAUNT	
"	11.9.15		CAPT D. MARR proceeded on leave this afternoon. A.D.M.S visited ambulance this afternoon 25 cars evacuated, formulating all the sick from the 7th Division	
"	12.9.15		Secret instructions received from A.D.M.S regarding arrangements for disposal B prisoners of war. Lt. R. CLARKE R.A.M.C joined for duty.	
"	13.9.15		33 evacuations including 22 cases of P.U.O.	
"	14.9.15		One N.C.O and 30 men sent to CHATEAU VERMELLES as a working party. 2 Officers 22 n 13 O.R evacuated to	
"	15.9.15		23 cars evacuated including 10 cases P.U.O. Sgt Major HUTCHENS joined for duty.	
"	16.9.15		Q.M.S HALFORD returned from No 9 C.C.S On discharge hospital to duty. Sgt STEER A.S.C ordered to report to 7th Div TRAIN for duty. Capt O'REILLY Lt. CLARKE took 30 bearers B Section proceeded to	
"	17.9.15		Capt O'REILLY Lt CLARKE took 30 bearers B Section proceeded to VERMELLES to take over A.D.S in from 22 n J.F.A. to evacuate wounded and sick from 7th DIV Trenches	
"	18.9.15		Received instructions from A.D.M.S to make arrangements to evacuate school now occupied by ambulance. As school will be required by the school authorities - orders were cancelled. D.D.M.S visited ambulance	

Army Form C. 2118

WAR DIARY
or
INTELLIGENCE SUMMARY
(Erase heading not required.)

Instructions regarding War Diaries and Intelligence Summaries are contained in F. S. Regs., Part II. and the Staff Manual respectively. Title Pages will be prepared in manuscript.

Place	Date	Hour	Summary of Events and Information	Remarks and references to Appendices
GONNEHEM	19.9.15		LT FORD R.A.M.C returned. LT HORROCKS as M.O½ WILTS RGT. Lt later proceeding on leave. Visited A.D.S.M + HULLOCK ALLEY.	
	20.9.15		CAPTAIN G. WRIGHT returned from leave and assumed command. Visited A.D.M.S. at his Office. In the afternoon visited D.S.M LE CHATEAU VERMELLES also A.D.S.m in the trenches.	
"	21.9.15		Attended conference in A.D.M.S Office at 12 noon. In the afternoon visited D.S.m VERMELLES. 15 cases were rested.	
"	22.9.15		Evacuating 77 Motoring our Officer. A.D.M.S visited ambulance.	
"	23.9.15		Received instructions from A.D.M.S to evacuate all cases not fit for duty in 2 hrs. O Annex. Received instructions from A.D.M.S - in atters. The Ambulance will march to sual Bivouac in the neighbourhood of FOUQUIERES main being e/routs to be made by 21st Infantry Bgde. Billets will not be availabile till 12 midnight on the 24th inst. The march may be carried out in daylight but when in Bivouac precautionary precautions for concealment from enemy aircraft will be taken. On the 23rd SEPTEMBER. The Ambulance will move to Le Sohut, LA BOURSE, to arrive there by 8 A.M. Visited A.Q.M.S and obtained permission for the ambulance to march by sections each section leaving at a different turn.	

WAR DIARY or INTELLIGENCE SUMMARY

Army Form C. 2118

Place	Date	Hour	Summary of Events and Information	Remarks and references to Appendices
GONNEHEM	24.9.15		B Section march at 10 a.m. for C Section move at 2 p.m. and A Section at 3.15 p.m. received all cars told the exception of 15 which were taken along with our advance. Sent to horse and company at LA BOURSE then completed by 5 p.m. Ambulance arrived in a field for the night at FOUQUIERES	
FOUGÈRES	25.9.15		Left FOUGUIÈRES at 6.15 a.m. and arrived at LA BOURSE Enemy shell at 9 a.m.	
LA BOURSE	26.9.15		On arrival found 8 schools occupied much improvements with A & Q to have schools emptied and handed over at 9.30 a.m. A.D.M.S. assisted ambulance and gave us instructions. We to spin until further orders. All motor ambulances and B & C Bearers sent to SAILLY LABOURSE & CHATEAU VERMELLES. One N.C.O. and two men sent to 4.30.9.4 on main BETHUNE–LENS road for the purpose of regulating the supply of ambulance waggons to D.C.S.M. at 12.15 p.m. received instructions from A.D.M.S. to open hospital in the schools as soon as possible to receive wounded. Hospital ready to receive wounded at 3.30 p.m. First wounded arrived at 3.40 p.m. Capt. MARR & Lt. WRIGHT sent to Advanced Coll Stn CHATEAU VERMELLES to assist. Ambulance visited by Surg. Gen. McPHERSON. At 9 p.m. received incidence from Capt. MACKIE and Lt. MILNE 23rd F.A. Number of wounded admitted from 4 p.m. – 12 mid. 300. Lt. F. McKIBBON left to join 16 R.W.F. 2nd Lt PETERS as M.O.	

Place	Date	Hour	Summary of Events and Information	Remarks and references to Appendices
LA BOURSE	26.9.15		Wounded continued to arrive all night & to specially stationed stretcher bearers, most of whom were very badly wounded and took a long time to dress. From 6 a.m. 25th inst. to 6 a.m. 26th inst. 3000 cases were admitted and wounded from Acknowed & @ Sn VERMELLES, several of these cases were only slightly wounded and were directed to walk to the Nearest Ambulance, there were opened track to BETHUNE in empty supply waggons and admitted to Field Ambulance cars there. Al I/P. M.C.D. @ Sn VERMELLES was clear of wounded. Our Motor Ambulance at a time was sent forward as far as possible up the HULLUCH road to evacuate wounded. At 3 p.m. Surg GEN MACPHERSON visited Ambulance. At 12 midday 4132 patients were in Hospital, between 12 midday and 3 p.m. 292 were evacuated. During the night the supply of stretchers ran short, patients were lifted off stretchers, so as to enable the Ambulances to run back with their proper supply of Lt stretchers. About 5 p.m. Col WESTCOTT visited Ambulance. The A.D.M.S visited the Ambulance several times. Received instructions from A.D.M.S that to evacuate slightly wounded and walking cases able to walk by M.A.C. Motor Cars to be sent to BETHUNE and transferred by train, 204 cases were transferred to BETHUNE by empty motor lorries.	

Army Form C. 2118

WAR DIARY
or
INTELLIGENCE SUMMARY
(Erase heading not required.)

Place	Date	Hour	Summary of Events and Information	Remarks and references to Appendices
LABOURSE	27/9/15		At 6 A.M received message from Act. Dir. Gen. Sm VERMELLES that Gen CAPPER was seriously wounded. During the afternoon that Capt. O'Reilly had taken him as P.O. 6 C.C. Hospital LILLERS. Several cases admitted to Hospital suffering from supposed gas poisoning. On examination no signs or symptoms could be detected, most of the cases were returned to duty. The wounded admitted not many from 2nd Div. Evacuation of wounded by 7th M.A.C. has been very good indeed. No of cases admitted from 6 A.M 26.9.15 to 6 A.M 27.9.15 = 432. Number evacuated 583. At 1.15 P.M CHATEAU VERMELLES Adv. of M.L. wounded. During the afternoon visited CHATEAU VERMELLES. The A.D.M.S. visited Ambulances several times. B Section 23rd F.A. opened their units. Admitted and evacuated from CHATEAU VERMELLES 700. Found Qn with mg. U., only 39 cases admitted during the night. Mail communication scarce.	
"	28.9.15		6 A.M. 27.9.15 - 147. Evacuations 262. Instructions received from D.M.S. 1st army that all cases as to be evacuated to BETHUNE. Number of cases admitted and evacuated from A.D. Col. Stn. 200. Ambulances visited by A.D.M.S and D.D.M.S 1st army.	

Army Form C. 2118

WAR DIARY
or
INTELLIGENCE SUMMARY
(Erase heading not required.)

Instructions regarding War Diaries and Intelligence Summaries are contained in F.S. Regs., Part II. and the Staff Manual respectively. Title Pages will be prepared in manuscript.

Place	Date	Hour	Summary of Events and Information	Remarks and references to Appendices
LABOURSE	29/9/15		Number of cases admitted from 66 MN (2DG-15) 49. Number discharged 36. Received instructions from A.D.M.S. to close Hospital and move from Labourse lock, Stk. — The Military and Civil Hospital BETHUNE. Hospital closed and ambulance ready to move at 2 p.m. B section transferred unit from Chateau VERMELLES. LT R. CLARKE left ambulance to join 2nd Yorks as M.O. Lt. J.V. BROUGHTON joined the ambulance for duty from No 16 General Hospital. Ambulance marched from LABOURSE at 4.40 p.m. and arrived at the Civil and Military Hospital BETHUNE 6.45 p.m. The Ambulance commenced packed all night.	
BETHUNE	30/9/15		Opened Hospital at 1 p.m. ready to receive wounded at Civil and Military Hospital. 4 teams transferred unit from CHATEAU VERMELLES. Fair hands of convalescence. Arrived at 1.30 p.m. A.D.M.S. visited ambulance.	

W.G. Wright
Capt R.A.M.C.
OC 2/1st West Mid.

30.9.15.

21/7429

7th Thorn

21st Field Ambulance
Oct X
Oct 15

Oct 15

WAR DIARY or INTELLIGENCE SUMMARY

Army Form C. 2118

Place	Date	Hour	Summary of Events and Information	Remarks and references to Appendices
BETHUNE	1/10/15		Over 60 wounded were admitted into Hospital during the night. O.C.S.M. who handed over to No 5 Field Ambulance 2nd Division. Capt D. Reilly and A. Sc. his teams rejoined at 11/0 A.M. Lt TORD rejoined for duty from 2" Bn WILTS. A.D.M.S. visited also the Ambulance.	
"	2.10.15		BETHUNE Stn Shelled. Received instructions to say that the 21st N/F Bde 2 WM Irish W Le Quesnoy and Ledretol in reserve. A.D.M.S. Suggested in the event of the Hospital being shelled the Ambulance should be moved to Church in Rue Pasteur. Sgt V/Sparks left this unit to join the 7" Div TRAIN as Cy S.M.S	
"	3.10.15		Received instructions from A.D.M.S. to take over the Advanced D.Sn from the 22" FA at LA-CAMBRIN. Capt JARDINE, R.A.M.C. and Lt BROUGHTON both A. section leaders took an Advanced Dressing station at CAMBRIN from 22" F.A. Two wounded admitted during the last 24 hours.	
"	3.10.15		Took over Officers theatre in the Civil and Military Hospital.	

WAR DIARY or INTELLIGENCE SUMMARY

(Erase heading not required.)

Army Form C. 2118

Instructions regarding War Diaries and Intelligence Summaries are contained in F.S. Regs., Part II. and the Staff Manual respectively. Title Pages will be prepared in manuscript.

21st FIELD AMBULANCE
7th DIVISION

Place	Date	Hour	Summary of Events and Information	Remarks and references to Appendices
BETHUNE	6.9.15		A.D.M.S. revisited the Ambulance. Inspected A.D.S. in the Convalescent Centre hoard at CAMBRIN.	
"	8.9.15		D.M.S. 1st Army and Col. LEISHMAN visited the Ambulance. The D.M.S. ordered the 6 Bd every with the present system of Retaining cases to be worked through the Hospital at Vie No. 130. C.C.S. Inspected Dressed System but No. 10.C.C.S. LAPUGNOY	
"	9.9.15		A.D.M.S. visited the Ambulance.	
"	10.10.15		Visited A.D.S. both D.A.D.M.S. 21st Inf. Bde. took over area occupied by the 20th Inf. 139R. A Section Bearers took over A.D.S. in WIMPOLE St. from 23rd F.A.	
"	12.10.15		SURG GEN MACPHERSON visited Ambulance to ascertain whether it turned take over another branch in the Hospital to an officers ward.	
"	13.10.15		20 wounded admitted and evacuated during the night. Between 5 & 6 p.m. two shells fell in the vicinity of the Hospital. A.D.M.S. visited Ambulance and suggested, in the event of having to move the Ambulance owing to shell fire, to move to ESSARS, all sick remaining to be transferred to the 23rd F.A. at ANNEQUIN.	
"	14.10.15		Two shells during the night. Inspected ESSAR with a view to forming Ambulance in Schools. CAPT. THEODINIE and A Section Bearers reported units from A.D.S. travelled over A.D.S. to 23rd F.A.	
"	15.10.15		Received two orderlies from A.D.M.S. to form the Ambulance Bearers to GONNEHEM.	

1

WAR DIARY or INTELLIGENCE SUMMARY

Army Form C. 2118

Place	Date	Hour	Summary of Events and Information	Remarks and references to Appendices
BETHUNE	16/10/15		At 8 A.M. B section marched. At 10 A.M. A & C sections marched arriving at GONNEHEM at 11.45 A.M. Died en route of pneumonia No 1 private A Swinbank Publishing, buried the 2nd Oct at Gonnehem. Funeral arrangements made to take over the Boys school on the 19th inst. At 12.9 p.m. secured ambulances from the 6.10 F.A.S. to move the two balance tomorrow to ST HILAIRE and 3 p.m.	
GONNEHEM	17/10/15		At 10 A.M. went over to St HILAIRE and arranged for hospital and billets etc.	
St HILAIRE	18/10/15		At 1 p.m. marched from GONNEHEM arriving St HILAIRE at 4.30 p.m. B m col a Hospital in a school room sufficient to take 50 cases. Capt O. RELLY has been transferred the Infantry Corps and R.M.S HALFORD to D.C.M. D.A.D.M.S visited the hospital and suggested if necessary Salter tops beds.	
"	19/10/15		From 4.30 p.m. all men were employed to billets wanting notice for the Ambulance to move. 8 cases transferred to the B.C.C.S AIRE	
"	20-10-15		Made arrangements for C Section complete to move into Civil and Military Hospital BETHUNE tomorrow morning at 8am.	
"	21.10.15		At 8.30 A.M. C section left with Capt QUANT for BETHUNE. Received orders for the whole Ambulance to move into Civil + Military Hospital BETHUNE A & C sections	
BETHUNE			left ST HILAIRE at 12 noon and marched to BETHUNE arriving at 5.45 p.m. Hospital (C section) open and ready to receive Sick and wounded at 1.15 p.m.	

WAR DIARY
or
INTELLIGENCE SUMMARY

Army Form C. 2118

Place	Date	Hour	Summary of Events and Information	Remarks and references to Appendices
BETHUNE	23/10/15		Received orders to take over A.D.S. at GIVENCHY from 23rd F.A. A.D.M.S. visited the Amb. interim.	
"	24/10/15		Capt. O'RELLY proceeded with C Section Orderlies and took over A.D.S. from 23rd F.A. Received orders to send LT. H.R. FORD to the 25th Div for duty in relief of Capt. W.K. FRY 2nd Div for duty with the 25th Div.	
"	25/10/15		LT H.R. FORD R.A.M.C. left today and proceeded to HAZEBROUCK to report to D.M.S. 2nd Div for duty with the 25th Div.	
"	26/10/15		Capt. MARR rejoined for duty on return of M.O. ¼ Cam from leave. A.D.M.S. visited the Ambulance.	
"	27/10/15		LT McKIBBEN R.A.M.C. joined this Unit for duty. Visited A.D.S. at LONE FARM.	
"	28/10/15		LT W.S. BAIRD proceeded on 8 days leave of absence. Received instructions from A.D.M.S. to hand over A.D.S. at LONE FARM to O.C. 22nd F.A. on the 29th inst.	
"	29/10/15		O.C. 7th Div Train inspected the transport and horses of the Ambulance. Capt. O'Reilly and C bearers rejoined. A.D.S. LONE FARM was handed over to 22nd F.A. at 2 p.m.	
"	30/10/15		5 cases of "Trench feet" from Cuinchy, in most cases the men had not their boots off for five days.	
"	31/10/15		A.D.M.S. visited Ambulance	

1/11/15

R. Pugh
Capt. Lt Col. R.A.M.C.
O.C. 21st Field Amb.

7th Karam

12/7637

Nov. 1915

21st Ind. Anur.
7
Nov 1915

Vol XI

WAR DIARY
INTELLIGENCE SUMMARY

Army Form C. 2118

Place	Date	Hour	Summary of Events and Information	Remarks and references to Appendices
BETHUNE	1/11/15		Received orders from A.D.M.S. to detail an Officer to relieve Lt HORROCKS as M.O. 1/2 2nd Bn WILTS. Capt McKIBBIN was detailed for duty and left to join the 2nd WILTS as M.O. 1/2	
"	2/11/15		LT. J.B. HORROCKS joined today for duty. A.D.M.S. visited the Ambulance.	
"	3/11/15		Received orders from A.D.M.S. that whole further notice the personnel of Field Amb. Workshops will do duty at the A.D.S. for transportable cases in town, belongs to be carried out in the 5 Coy	
"	5/11/15		Capt O'REILLY and LT BROUGHTON with B section Horse proceeded to LONE FARM and 1stR on A.D.S. from the 23rd F.A. CAPT JARDINE returned from leave. A.D.M.S. visited the Ambulance on A.D.S. at PONT FIXE.	
"	6/11/15		Visited A.D.S. and made arrangements to open a dressing room at PONT FIXE.	
"	7/11/15		D.A.D.M.S. inspected A.D.S. and Dressing Room at 2/2nd F.A. on the Q'd visit.	
"	8/11/15		Received instructions to hand over A.D.S. to 22nd F.A. B section reported unit.	
"	9/11/15		A.D.S. LONE FARM handed over to 22nd F.A. B section Horses reported unit. CAPT O'REILLY proceeded on leave of absence.	
"	10/11/15		LT BAIRD proceeded on temporary duty as M.O. 1/2 26 " Bty " R.G.A. during absence of M.O. on leave.	
"	11/11/15		LT BROUGHTON proceeded on temporary duty as M.O. 1/2 2nd YORKS to replace LT CLARKE. A.D.M.S. inspected the Ambulance at 3 P.M. LT CLARKE joined this unit for duty from M.O. 1/2 2nd YORKS.	

Army Form C. 2118

WAR DIARY
or
INTELLIGENCE SUMMARY
(Erase heading not required.)

Instructions regarding War Diaries and Intelligence Summaries are contained in F.S. Regs., Part II. and the Staff Manual respectively. Title Pages will be prepared in manuscript.

Place	Date	Hour	Summary of Events and Information	Remarks and references to Appendices
BETHUNE	12/1/15		Capt E. GAUNT proceeded on leave. LT B. WRIGHT	
"	13/1/15		On M.O.'s Chuing the absence of LT AMYOT sick in hospital. A.D.M.S visited the ambulance.	
"	14/1/15		Received instructions from A.D.M.S to take over A.D.S. LONE FARM from O.C. 23rd F.A. on the 16th inst.	
"	16/1/15		Capt JARDINE + LT HORROCKS took over A.D.S LONE FARM from 23rd F.A. also took over Post preparation room at ESSARS + LE QUESNOY and PONT FIXE. LT WICKERSHAM proceeded on leave. Visited A.D.S LONE FARM.	
"	18/1/15		Opened dressing room at LE QUESNOY + ESSARS.	
"	19/1/15		Received instructions from A.D.M.S to open post preparation rooms in 5 farmhouses and pros at WINDY CORNER and to reinforce the room at PONT FIXE.	
"	21/1/15		At 2:30 pm GEN. WATTS inspected the ambulance. A.D.M.S visited the ambulance. LT W.S. BAIRD reported unit for duty. Visited A.D.S LONE FARM.	
"	22/1/15		LT GARROD Joined the ambulance for instruction. A.D.M.S visited the ambulance.	
"	24/1/15		LT GARROD joined the ambulance for instruction. Brigade from 100th F.A. A.D.M.S visited the ambulance.	
"	25/1/15		CAPT GAUNT returned off leave. LT CLARK who went there sick	

Army Form C. 2118

WAR DIARY
or
INTELLIGENCE SUMMARY
(Erase heading not required.)

Instructions regarding War Diaries and Intelligence Summaries are contained in F. S. Regs., Part II. and the Staff Manual respectively. Title Pages will be prepared in manuscript.

Place	Date	Hour	Summary of Events and Information	Remarks and references to Appendices
BETHUNE	27.11.14		D.M.S. 1st Army held a conference at this hospital.	
"	28.11.14		Received instructions from A.D.M.S. to hand over the Corps Field Hospital, A.D.S. LONE FARM For preparation rooms at ESSARS & LE QUESNOY to O.C. 19th F.A. on the 30th inst. or the 1st Dec. The ambulance will then to BERGUETTE and open up.	
"	30.11.14		Attended conference at A.D.M.S. Office. Lt AMYOT was sent down sick. Received instructions from B.S.F.E. postponing all move for 24 hours.	

R.L. Boyle
Lt.Col R.A.M.C
O.C. 21st F.A.

1.12.15-

21·ii·72 Auls.

Do / vol. XII

Do

F/130/11

Dec. 1915

Army Form C. 2118

WAR DIARY
or
INTELLIGENCE SUMMARY
(Erase heading not required.)

Instructions regarding War Diaries and Intelligence Summaries are contained in F.S. Regs., Part II. and the Staff Manual respectively. Title Pages will be prepared in manuscript.

Place	Date	Hour	Summary of Events and Information	Remarks and references to Appendices
BETHUNE	1/12/15		Handed over Clric & Mil Hosp, A.O.S LONE FARM. 91st prep motor amm. at Lt DUBOIS & ESSARS to OC 19th F.A. Capt GAUNT with A-B Sections proceeded to BERGUETTE and formed B Section in school.	
"	2/12/15		C Section left and proceeded to BERGUETTE.	
BERGUETTE	3/12/15		Capt MARR proceeded to H/q Camerons as M.O./c in place of Lt WOODS (wounded). Attached bon parce at A.D.M.S. Office. Received instructions from A.D.M.S. to send forward a Walking party to LE MESGE and two motor ambulances.	
"	4/12/15		Lt BAIRD with advance party proceeded to LE MESGE.	
"	6/12/15		Received instructions to entrain at BERGUETTE on 6th inst at 7.21 p.m. Evacuated all sick and closed Hospital at 12.30 p.m. At 4.30 p.m. left to entrain at Station, we trained in 40 minutes. Left BERGUETTE SLN at 7.21 p.m. and arrived at PONT-REMY (AMIENS Map) at 3 A.M. (7.12.15)	AMIENS MAP
PONT REMY	7/12/15		Commenced detraining at 3.55 A.M. detrained in one hour. Left PONT-REMY at 5.30 a.m. to mard to LE MESGE arriving at 9 A.S.G.M. A section formed at.	
LE MESGE			MAISON A VENDRE DE LALLER, LE MESGE. Hospital open and ready to receive Sick at 3 p.m.	

Army Form C. 2118

WAR DIARY
or
INTELLIGENCE SUMMARY
(Erase heading not required.)

Instructions regarding War Diaries and Intelligence Summaries are contained in F.S. Regs., Part II. and the Staff Manual respectively. Title Pages will be prepared in manuscript.

Place	Date	Hour	Summary of Events and Information	Remarks and references to Appendices
LE MESGE	8/12/15		Capt MARR rejoined from 1/4 CAMERONS. Capt LYONS R.A.M.C. joined for duty from the 2/1 GEN. Hospital. 5 men transferred to M.M. C.C.S. AMIENS. D.A.D.M.S. visited the MM. Ambulance.	
"	10/12/15		Attended a conference at the A.D.M.S. Office. Received instructions from A.D.M.S. to send all men, except skin cases, to the 23rd F.A. at PICQUIGNY. 22 men were sent to the 23rd F.A.	
"	12/12/15		4384 Sgt L.S.G. TURNER proceeded to G.H.Q. for duty. Lt. G. HORROCKS proceeded to England to report to W.O. on completion of two years hon. contract.	
"	13/12/15		Lt BROUGHTON proceeded on temporary duty in M.O/C 1st Bty. R.H.A. to replace Capt NELSON during his absence on leave. Lt WRIGHT returned from leave.	
"	16/12/15		D.A.D.M.S. visited the Mm Ambulance.	
"	17/12/15		Sgt. BERRY joined for duty from G.H.Q. Lt WRIGHT proceeded to 2nd B.E.D.S.	
"	18/12/15		On temporary duty during the absence of Lt AMYOT on leave.	
"	19/12/15		Capt LYONS joined the 2 YORKS as M.O/C for duty on and during 2 Willes & YORKS left the Bde to join the 30th Div.	

Army Form C. 2118

WAR DIARY
or
INTELLIGENCE SUMMARY
(Erase heading not required.)

No. 21 Field Ambulance

Instructions regarding War Diaries and Intelligence Summaries are contained in F.S. Regs., Part II. and the Staff Manual respectively. Title Pages will be prepared in manuscript.

Place	Date	Hour	Summary of Events and Information	Remarks and references to Appendices
LE MESGE	20.12.15		21st & 22nd MANCHESTERs 1st SOUTH STAFFORDS + 2nd QUEENS joined the Bgde	
	21.12.15		A.D.M.S. visited the Ambulance.	
	22.12.15		Attended Conference at A.D.M.S Office.	
	25.12.15		R.M.O. HALFORD left to join the 1/2nd C.C.S at Heure as Orderly Officer	
	26.12.15		Lt BROUGHTON returned from 14th 13th T.H.A.	
			CAPT MARR proceeded on leave	
	28.12.15		Lt BROUGHTON posted to 7th Div Ammn Col for temporary duty.	
	29.12.15		Attended conference at A.D.M.S Office	
	30.12.15		CAPT E.B. JARDINE forwarded to 1/1st SOUTH STAFFORDS for temporary duty.	
	31.12.15			

1st Jan 1916

W L Bright
Capt R.A.M.C
O=C. 21 F.A.

4

21 Ja Aust.
Jan
Vol XIII

Y. H. Duncan

P/130/2

Jan 1918.

S1

Army Form C. 2118

ORIGINAL.

WAR DIARY
or
INTELLIGENCE SUMMARY
(Erase heading not required.)

Instructions regarding War Diaries and Intelligence Summaries are contained in F.S. Regs., Part II. and the Staff Manual respectively. Title Pages will be prepared in manuscript.

Place	Date	Hour	Summary of Events and Information	Remarks and references to Appendices
LE MESGE	2.1.16		Lt B. WRIGHT returned from 1st BEDFORDS.	
"	3.1.16		A.D.M.S visited the Ambulance.	
"	4.1.16		D.D.M.S visited the Hospital.	
"	6.1.16		O.C 21st F.A. proceeded on leave.	
"	7.1.16		Capt. D.M. MARR returned from leave.	
"	10.1.16		Lt BROUGHTON returned from temp duty Lt 7th Div. Am. Col.	
"	19.1.16		A.D.M.S visited the Ambulance.	
"	24.1.16		O.C 21st F.A returned from leave.	
"	27.1.16		O.C 7th Div TRAIN inspected all the transport.	
"	28.1.16		A.D.M.G, 13th Corps visited the Ambulance. Capt. D BALLINGALL N.R.M.C. joined for duty from FD 2nd R.E. Capt J.B. JARDINE joined from temp duty with 1st South Staffs	
"	29.1.16		Received orders from FD 2nd 91st Inf Bgd 13.9.85 for the Am btance to proceed to CADONNETTE on the 30 Jan't.	
"	30.1.16		Left LE MESGE at 8.30 a.m Arrived at CADONNETTE at 4 p.m.	

Army Form C. 2118

ORIGINAL

WAR DIARY
or
INTELLIGENCE SUMMARY

(Erase heading not required.)

Instructions regarding War Diaries and Intelligence Summaries are contained in F. S. Regs., Part II. and the Staff Manual respectively. Title Pages will be prepared in manuscript.

Place	Date	Hour	Summary of Events and Information	Remarks and references to Appendices
CARDONNETTE CORBIE	3/1/16		Left CARDONNETTE at 10 a.m. and marched to CORBIE arriving at 2.30 p.m. Received orders from A.D.M.S. to proceed to Sailly LAURETTE and take over billets from No 13 Field Ambulance, the Ambulance to remain closed except for local sick.	

B. T. Long
Capt. R.A.M.C.
O.C. 21st F.A.

In the Field
1st Feb 1916

~~4th Div~~

21st. Field Amb.

S Feb. / 1916
S Mar. /
S /

Army Form C. 2118

WAR DIARY
OF
INTELLIGENCE SUMMARY
(Erase heading not required.)

Instructions regarding War Diaries and Intelligence Summaries are contained in F.S. Regs., Part II. and the Staff Manual respectively. Title Pages will be prepared in manuscript.

Place	Date	Hour	Summary of Events and Information	Remarks and references to Appendices
CORBIE	1/2/16		Received orders from 91st Bgde Hd Qrs for the Amb. Sect. ones to proceed to SAILLY LAURETTE on the 2nd inst.	
"	2/2/16		Left CORBIE at 10.30 A.M. arrived at SAILLY LAURETTE 12.30 P.M. Received instructions from A.D.M.S. to open up A.D.S. if necessary. Sent motor ambulances from A.D.M.S. to take over A.D.S. at BRAY on the 3rd inst. from 23rd F.A.	
SAILLY LAURETTE	3/2/16		CAPT. O'REILLY with B.S.ns. heavies left at M.G. for front proceeded to BRAY and took over A.D.S. from 23rd F.A. at the CITADEL with D.S. at BRAY. Took over the A.D.S. tent posted as he took Sq. proc. Pvt. M.C.D. last visit 1334. Then ordered CAPT. O'REILLY to enlarge to front out A.D.S. at the CITADEL and to move one Sec. M.A. Conv., LT. BROUGHTON to take over charge of D.S. at BRAY.	
"	4/2/16		At 5 P.M. D.S. at BRAY.	
"	6/2/16		Started D.S. at BRAY. Took on billets vacated by the 13th F.A. Opened small A.D. Bath pool. Drains D.S. at BRAY.	

WAR DIARY
OF
INTELLIGENCE SUMMARY

(Erase heading not required.)

Army Form C. 2118

Instructions regarding War Diaries and Intelligence Summaries are contained in F. S. Regs., Part II. and the Staff Manual respectively. Title Pages will be prepared in manuscript.

Place	Date	Hour	Summary of Events and Information	Remarks and references to Appendices
SACILLY LAURETTE	7/2/16		A.D.M.S visited the Ambulance. Took on Similary change of the village of SAILLY LAURETTE	
"	8/2/16		A.D.M.S visited O.S at BRAY and A.D.S at The CITADEL.	
"	9/2/16		Visited D.S at BRAY. Arranged sketch map & census for wounded in the event of heavy shelling.	
"	11/2/16		Lt BAIRD proceeded on 10 days leave, from 16 Manchesters. Posted this ambulance in the 22nd inst. Moving to the Front side of Lt BRAY CORBIE road, made arrangements to evacuate sick & wounded by Horse Ambulance to SAILLY LAURETTE, It is quite impossible to have the Motor Ambulance on this road at night. Visited 91st Bgde 7th Dvn	
"	12/2/16		Inspected SAILLY les Sec and VAUX with the A.D.M.S on our to Front to have fun the Ambulance to Spring Mo Bricklaying & Ovences for a F.A.	
"	13/2/16		CAPT. D. MARR proceeded on temps. duty to M.O/c 21st MANCHESTERS Lt FULLERTON R.A.M.C. Joined for temp. duty from 21st MANCHESTERS	

Army Form C. 2118

WAR DIARY
OF
INTELLIGENCE SUMMARY
(Erase heading not required.)

Instructions regarding War Diaries and Intelligence Summaries are contained in F. S. Regs., Part II. and the Staff Manual respectively. Title Pages will be prepared in manuscript.

Place	Date	Hour	Summary of Events and Information	Remarks and references to Appendices
SHELLY LAURETTE	16.2.16		A.D.M.S visited the Ambulance.	
"	17.2.16		D.D.M.S 13th CORPS visited the Ambulance. Lt FULLERTON. R.A.M.C. proceeded to ROUEN for duty.	
"	20.2.16		Bye drying Room opened at BRAY. CAPT BALLINGAL took over charge of A.D.S BRAY + CAPT JARDINE A.D.S at the CITADEL. LAPT O'REILLY + LT BROUGHTON R/mid at 9d 2 Bn. LT WICKERSHAM proceeded in Leave.	
"	22.2.16		D.A.D.M.S visited the Ambulance	
"	23.2.16		Visited BRAY. A.D.S CITADEL R.A.Ps Jn. Sectn Q.1 + C.11 took D.A.D.M.S. Capt Ballingall was relieved at A.D.S BRAY by LT WRIGHT.	
"	24.2.16		Capt BALLINGALL proceeded on leave.	
"	26.2.16		G.O.C XIII CORPs visited the Ambulance. ADMS. D.A.D.M.S visited the Ambulance. A.D.S BRAY. Between 9.50 p.m & g several shells dropped by the A.D.S BRAY hitting two M. Ambulances.	
"	27.2.16		formed an establishment 65 beds for by the cases in the schools. 1 N.C.O + 8 men sent to BRONFERM to collect wounded from Sectn B.111. 28/2/16	

4

21 Ja Acub
Vol XV

WAR DIARY
or
INTELLIGENCE SUMMARY
(Erase heading not required.)

Army Form C. 2118

Instructions regarding War Diaries and Intelligence Summaries are contained in F. S. Regs., Part II. and the Staff Manual respectively. Title Pages will be prepared in manuscript.

Place	Date	Hour	Summary of Events and Information	Remarks and references to Appendices
SAILLY LAURETTE	1.3.16		LT G COOPER and LT FELDMAN joined for duty from 14 GENERAL	
	2.3.16		LT G COOPER proceeded to the CITADEL for duty.	
"	8.3.16		Received instructions from A.D.M.S. to be prepared to move the Ambulance to REBEMONT on the 6th inst. LT WICKERSHAM returned from leave. Visited A.D.M.S.	
"	6.3.16		C Section with CAPT. E. GAUNT proceeded to RIBEMONT. Received instructions from A.D.M.S. not to move the ambulance from here. Closed hospital at SAILLY LAURETTE	
	7.3.16		A + B Sections proceeded to RIBEMONT. Arrived at CHATEAU RIBEMONT. Hospital opened ready to receive sick and wounded at 4 P.M.	
RIBEMONT	8.3.16		A.D.M.S. visited the Ambulance. Received instructions that 16 D.M.S IV ARMY would visit the Ambulance tomorrow. Arrange the G.S. wagons + transport & hire horses.	
"	9.3.16		Col 2nd I.M.S IV Army visited the Ambulance. CAPT E. GAUNT proceeded 6th M.A.C for duty as I.O.P.C. A.D.M.S. visited the Ambulance.	
"	11.3.16 15.3.16		CAPT BALLINGALL proceeded to the CITADEL for duty. LT COOPER returning at H.Q. Ars.	

WAR DIARY or INTELLIGENCE SUMMARY

Army Form C. 2118

(Erase heading not required.)

Instructions regarding War Diaries and Intelligence Summaries are contained in F.S. Regs., Part II. and the Staff Manual respectively. Title Pages will be prepared in manuscript.

Place	Date	Hour	Summary of Events and Information	Remarks and references to Appendices
RIBEMONT	20.3.16		A.D.M.S. visited the Ambulance. Lt COOPER proceeded on temp M.O/c 2/4th MANCHESTERS in relief of Capt MARR who rejoined 9th F.A.	
"	21.3.16		D.A.D.M.S. XIII Corps visited the Ambulance	
"	23.3.16		Capt DALLINGALL proceeded on temp duty as D.A.D.M.S. 30th Div. Visited A.D.S. BRAY with D.A.D.M.S.	
"	24.3.16			
"	27.3.16		LT WRIGHT joined 7th D.A.C. as M.O/c. LT VOYCE R.A.M.C. joined for duty from 18th Genl Base.	
"	28.3.16		A.D.M.S. visited the Ambulance. CAPT JARDINE proceeded on leave.	
"	29.3.16		Received instructions from A.D.M.S. to chief hospital and to move from the Ambulance to CORBIE on the 30th inst. to be known as Ridemont [?] by 6 p.m. on the 30th inst.	
"	30.3.16		Closed hospital. Marched from RIBEMONT al. 3 p.m. arriving at CORBIE at 4.45 p.m. Did not open up the Ambulance but sick & wounded are being sent to 23rd F.A. at MERICOURT	

31/3/16

B.T. [signature]
Major O.C. 2/1st [?]

№ IV 4th Division

№. 21 F. Amb.

April 1915.

5

COMMITTEE FOR THE
MEDICAL HISTORY OF THE WAR
Date 9 - JUN. 1915

Army Form C. 2118

No. 21 Field Ambulance.

WAR DIARY
or
INTELLIGENCE SUMMARY
(Erase heading not required.)

Instructions regarding War Diaries and Intelligence Summaries are contained in F.S. Regs., Part II. and the Staff Manual respectively. Title Pages will be prepared in manuscript.

Place	Date	Hour	Summary of Events and Information	Remarks and references to Appendices
CORBIE	1/4/16		Lt COOPER proceeded to join 2nd GORDONS as M.O i/c Field Hospital	
"	3/4/16		A.D.M.S visited the Ambulance. Lt P.K.G McKENZIE joined for duty from No 9 GENERAL	
"	4/4/16		O.C 7 Div Train inspected the transport	
"	6/4/16		CAPT L.T. O'REILLY proceeded on leave	
	7/4/16		Took on Officers Rest Station from the 23rd F.A. Capt E.B JARDINE returned from leave	
	9/4/16		Sgt Maj PACKER A.S.C joined for duty from 7th Div TRAIN	
	10/4/16		Lt A. BARRETT R.A.M.C joined for duty from No 20 GENERAL	
	11/4/16		CAPT JARDINE proceeded to the CITADEL + took over from LT BROUGHTON who rejoined H.Q. Rd	
	13/4/16		Received instructions from A.D.M.S to handover the A.D.S at BRAY + CITADEL to the 23rd F.A. The move to be completed by the 18th inst. All leave stopped + all Officers + men to be recalled	

Army Form C. 2118

WAR DIARY
or
INTELLIGENCE SUMMARY
(Erase heading not required.)

No. 21 Field Ambulance

Instructions regarding War Diaries and Intelligence Summaries are contained in F.S. Regs, Part II. and the Staff Manual respectively. Title Pages will be prepared in manuscript.

Place	Date	Hour	Summary of Events and Information	Remarks and references to Appendices
CORBIE	14.4.16		Lt JOYCE rejoined FA 20 from the CITADEL. A.D.M.S visited the Ambulance.	
"	15.4.16		Handed over A.D.S at BRAY to the 23rd F.A. Lt FELDMAN + 8 men rejoined FA 28 from A.D.S BRAY.	
"	16.4.16		CAPT JARDINE transferred from A.D.S CITADEL to the 23rd F.A. + 8 men to 20 Bns.	
"	18.4.16 24.4.16 25.4.16		CAPT O'REILLY returned from leave. Lt BROUGHTON seconded as Temp.Staff in M.O. ½ 26th MANCHESTERS. Received instructions from O.C. No. 5 to move the Ambulance from CORBIE to MORLANCOURT on the 27th inst. ready to close the Offices Rail Stn on the 27th inst.	
"	26.4.16		A.D.M.S visited the Ambulance.	
"	27.4.16		Cloud Sprin R.A.L.Stn, 1st Officers (BP) were returned to 21 C.C.S.	
MORLANCOURT	28.4.16		Marched from CORBIE at 1.40 p.m. Ambulance vans were cleared. Full sick up. One Sentry returned to the 23rd F.A. at MERICOURT. Received instructions from A.D.M.S to take over the camps in the BRAY-CORBIE Road from Lt 20' F.A.	
"	29.4.16		Took over camps on the BRAY-CORBIE Road from E 20' F.A. Lt McKENZIE joined from duty from 1st Scott Staffs.	

30th April 1916
R.G. Tong Lt Col
Comdg No 21 F.A.

1st Div.

No. 21 7. Arat.

May 19/16.
S/

COMMITTEE FOR THE
MEDICAL HISTORY OF THE WAR
Date 26 JUN 1916

WAR DIARY or INTELLIGENCE SUMMARY

Army Form C. 2118.

No. 21 FIELD AMBULANCE

Vol 17

Place	Date	Hour	Summary of Events and Information	Remarks and references to Appendices
BRAY CORBIE Road. @ K21.D.8.9.	1/5/16		Moved from MORLANCOURT to BRAY-CORBIE Road K21.D.8.9. Ref map ALBERT 1/40000	Ref Map ALBERT 1/10000
	2/5/16		Dict and gym supplied. O.O.C XIII Corps visited the camp.	
	3/5/16		D.A.D.M.S. visited the camp.	
	4/5/16		Lt JOYCE proceeded on tempy duty to M.O/c 2nd QUEENS	
			O.D.M.S. XV Corps visited the camp. Visit Gen the two mechanics to shew neary self the shaft	
			+ took the mechanics were examines the 5th ment. Wd 11.30 p.m. received word during from D.A.D.M.S.	
			and to move the Ambulance next night to be frowned the XV Corps on the completion of stay.	
			Orders received. When he was word that to France	
	7/5/16		Lt McKENZIE proceeded to England on completion of tour Gen med.	
			Moved Ambulance to MORLANCOURT. Dict with from	
MORLANCOURT	8/5/16		3 N.C.O.s + 50 men proceeded to No 38 C.C.S. on tempy duty. D.A.D.M.S. visited the Ambulance	
"	11/5/16		Lt BROUGHTON wound from temp duty with 2/6 MANCHESTERS.	
"	12/5/16		Lt BROUGHTON proceeded on tempy duty. 1 N.C.O. + 25 men proceeded to No 38 C.C.S. on tempy duty.	
"	14/5/16		Lt FELDMAN R.A.M.C. + 3 men proceeded to Corps Cav HQ 2/o HEILLY for duty	
	15/5/16		Formed a stace 20 Bed Red Hospital in the camp.	
"	17/5/16		Lt JOYCE Returned from tempy duty with the 2" QUEENS	
	18/5/16		D.A.D.M.S. wded that the Ambulance no M.O/c 22 Bty R.F.A.	
	19/5/16		Lt BARRETT proceeded on tempy duty	

WAR DIARY No. 21 FIELD AMBULANCE
or
INTELLIGENCE SUMMARY

Army Form C. 2118

(Erase heading not required.)

Place	Date	Hour	Summary of Events and Information	Remarks and references to Appendices
MORLANCOURT	22/5/16		CAPT D MARR forwarded to H.Q. 2nd IV Army for a course in Anti Gas Appliances.	ALBERT 1/40000
"	23/5/16		LT VOYCE forwarded to 21st MANCHESTERS on temp duty.	
"	24/5/16		A.D.M.S. visited the Amb billets.	
"	25/5/16		LT FELDMAN rejoined for duty from the XV Corps.	
"	28/5/16		CAPT. D. MARR rejoined H.Q. from Anti Gas School. CAPT BROUGHTON rejoined from Leave.	
"	29/5/16		LT BARRETT rejoined from 22/13 Bde R.F.A.	
"	31/5/16		CAPT. D. BALLINGALL R.G.M.C. appointed D.A.D.M.S. 30th Div and is struck off the strength of this unit	

Ja Ob Pulled
31/5/16

[signature]
Major R.A.M.C.
OC 21st F.A.

No. 21 Field Ambulance

7th D[iv]

June 1916

Army Form C. 2118

No 21 FIELD AMBULANCES

Vol 18

WAR DIARY
or
INTELLIGENCE SUMMARY
(Erase heading not required.)

Instructions regarding War Diaries and Intelligence Summaries are contained in F. S. Regs., Part II. and the Staff Manual respectively. Title Pages will be prepared in manuscript.

Place	Date	Hour	Summary of Events and Information	Remarks and references to Appendices
MORLANCOURT	1/8/16		Major W. G. Wright RAMC proceeded on short leave	
	2/8/16		D.A.D.M.S. visited the ambulance	
	3/8/16		Hon Lieut- R.W. J. Wickersham R.A.M.C. proceeded to 45 C.C.S. for duty	
	4/8/16		Hon Lieut- R.W. T.A. GRIGGS joined this ambulance for duty from 45 C.C.S. Lieut- I FELDMAN left for inoculation duty with 14th Heavy Artillery Group. Lieut- C.R. JOYCE rejoined from temporary duty with 21st Manchester Regiment. D.D.M.S. XV Corps visited the ambulance and asked me to be in readiness for an inspection by the G.O.C. XV Corps to-morrow	
	6/8/16		G.O.C. XV Corps inspected the Ambulance	
	7/8/16		A.D.M.S. visited the ambulance	
	8/8/16		Lieut- C.R. Joyce left for temporary duty with Divl Sanitary Officer	
	10/8/16		Allocated new field for hospital and proceeded to have it hepped out	

Army Form C. 2118.

WAR DIARY
or
INTELLIGENCE SUMMARY
(Erase heading not required.)

No. 21 FIELD AMBULANCE

Place	Date	Hour	Summary of Events and Information	Remarks and references to Appendices
MORLANCOURT	11/6/16		A.D.M.S. & D.A.D.M.S. visited the ambulance. Lieut. O.R. Joyce R.A.M.C. rejoined from Sanitary Section. Lieut. A. Barrett R.A.M.C. proceeded to 21st Manchester Regt. for temporary duty.	
	12/6/16		O.C. returned from leave.	
	13/6/16		Capt. D. Marr promoted on leave. A.D.M.S. visited the ambulance. Capt. McMillan joined for duty from No. 25 Sta. Hospital.	
	16/6/16		D.D.M.S. XV Corps visited the ambulance.	
	17/6/16		Capt. Dowzer joined for duty from the 23rd F.A.	
	19/6/16		A.D.M.S. visited the ambulance.	
	20/6/16		Surg. Genl. MacPherson & D.D.M.S. XV Corps visited the ambulance.	
	23/6/16		Capt. D. Marr returned from leave. A.D.M.S. visited the ambulance. Received instructions from the A.D.M.S. to take in and send a return that the ambulance is taken on the Bray-Meaulte Road Capt. E.B. Vardenes took over from Capt. to D.C.S. + 30 men joined that to D.C.S.	
	24/6/16		D.D.M.S. XV Corps visited the ambulance + D.C.S.	

Army Form C. 2118

WAR DIARY
or
INTELLIGENCE SUMMARY No 21 FIELD AMBULANCE
(Erase heading not required.)

Instructions regarding War Diaries and Intelligence Summaries are contained in F.S. Regs., Part II. and the Staff Manual respectively. Title Pages will be prepared in manuscript.

Place	Date	Hour	Summary of Events and Information	Remarks and references to Appendices
MARLANCOURT	25/6/16		D.G + D.M.S IV ARMY visited Us and to camp.	
"	26/6/16		Lt Joyce posted to No 5 C.C.S on temp duty.	
"	27/6/16		D.D.M.S XV Corps visited Us from Bulcourt.	
"	28/6/16		O.D.C XV Corps visited Us from Bulcourt.	
"	29/6/16		D.D.M.S XV Corps visited the new bivouac	
"	30/6/16		at B Dresser Stations posted chief to MINDEN POST + C Station 6 at CITADEL 12 Med Cars belonging to 20 Divn Borrowed 6 D.C.S + 6 sent to Capt VARDICARS for chy.	

For the RAMC
1-7-16

B.T. Esq K
Mag Abt C
Ty 21.06 FA

Daly GSHQ 3rd Echelon.

With reference to B.G.M.S. G.H.Q. No. 371/1, dated 28.6.16, I beg to report that no Australians, Canadians or New Zealanders have been treated in this unit from January 1916 to the present date.

Major R____
O/C 21st F.A.

4th Division

No 21 Field Ambulance

July 1916.
S

COMMITTEE FOR THE
MEDICAL HISTORY OF THE W
Date 13 SEP 1915

WAR DIARY No. 21 FIELD AMBULANCE. Army Form C. 2118
or
INTELLIGENCE SUMMARY JULY 1916
(Erase heading not required.)

Appx 19

Place	Date	Hour	Summary of Events and Information	Remarks and references to Appendices
MORLANCOURT	1/7/16		At 7.30 A.M. the attack commenced. 30 M.A.C. (27) Cars arrived at 11.30 A.M. The first wounded arrived at 9 A.M. By 12 noon 30 cars were admitted. Surg. Gen. MACPHERSON visited the ambulance. The wounded arrived steadily all day. Total number admitted from 6 A.M. - 8 A.M. Officers 36. O.R. 489. Germans 26. Total = 529. Upto 8 P.M. lying cases D.D.M.S. XV Corps visited between. All cases were evacuated to 38 + 5 C.C.S.	
"	2/7/16		At 2 A.M. received information that two more cases were to be evacuated while further orders. During the night admitted about 70 sitting cases from 23rd F.A. Remaining at 6 A.M. O.O O.R. (Inj?) 272 Sitting G. Prisoners 17. At 6 A.M. received instructions to evacuate the 100 cases B.S.M. C.C.S. AMIENS + 36 to 36 C.C.S. 130 lying cases admitted between 8 A.M & 12 noon. At 11.6 A.M. received instructions that 36+39 C.C.S were open. 194 lying admitted from 12 noon - 6 P.M. Evacuation continued steadily. At 6 C. 1881 the receiving J.PO German horse had 15 cases release cases slower. By 4.30 A.M. Col 7 A.M. Jr O.C. F.A. arrived that new motoring J it German overrun shed. O.D.M.S. XV Corps visited between relieved. Total 56 - 36 C.C.M. 40 O.R. 129. G. Anis 1196. 2147	
"	3/7/16		Very quiet day. Only 13 cases evacuated from 6.6. A.M. - 6 P.M. Ambulance kept clear. All day Pol 4.30 P.M. evacuated 60 Germans to the Corps	

WAR DIARY
or
INTELLIGENCE SUMMARY

(Erase heading not required.)

Army Form C. 2118.

No 74 FIELD AMBULANCE
JULY 1916

Place	Date	Hour	Summary of Events and Information	Remarks and references to Appendices
MORLANCOURT	4/7/16		Very quiet day. Only 6 cases admitted from 6 p.m. (3rd) – 6 a.m. Lt J.R. McKENZIE joined for duty from No 2 Staf Hosp. 3 Officers + 36 men adms. Unit from 6 a.m – 6 p.m. Received no wounded from the A.D.M.S. to withdraw 2 of the teams from U D.C.S D.D.M.S XV Corps visited the unit today.	
	5/7/16		Admitted from 6 p.m. (4th) – 6 a.m. 14. Very quiet day. Received no wounded. from the A.D.M.S. to withdraw all my teams to hand over the D.C.S.6. Lt 13 D/S F.A. Corps E 13. Jardine having handed over the D.C.S. 9 an ut W.D.) 25. Admitted from 6 a.m. – 6 p.m. 7 Officers + 5 O.R.	
	6/7/16		Admitted from 6 p.m. (5th) to 6 a.m. 3 Officers – 17 O.R. Received instructions from A.D.M.S. that the Ambulance will now run from AL MORIANCOURT + will be Hosp. attached to the 30th Div. to take v sicks. All by war in chl. Admitted from 6 a.m. – 6 p.m. 2 Off 2 O.R.	
	7/7/16		Admitted from 6 p.m. (6th) – 6 a.m. 2 Off 2 O.R. 6 a.m. – 6 p.m. 1 Off 16 O.R. SURG GEN MACPHERSON + D.M.S. IV Corps visited the Ambulance	

WAR DIARY
or
INTELLIGENCE SUMMARY

(Erase heading not required.)

Army Form C. 2118.

No. 21 FIELD AMBULANCE

July 1916.

Place	Date	Hour	Summary of Events and Information	Remarks and references to Appendices
MORLANCOURT	8.7.16		Admitted from 6 p.m.(7) - 6 A.M. 41 Off + 21 O.R. Admitted from 6 A.M. - 6 P.M. 13 Off/720 + 7 O.R. D.D.M.S. XV Corps visited us this Interview.	
	9.7.16		Admitted from 6 p.m.(D) - 6 A.M. 3 Off + 33. O.R. Admitted from 6 A.M. - 6 P.M. 5 Off + 76. O.R.	
	10.7.16		Admitted from 6 p.m.(9) - 6 A.M. 8. O.R. Admitted from 6 A.M. - 6 P.M. 38 Off + 174. O.R. 20 Germans admitted Capt. VARDINIE + 4 Sec. transferred to the ORCHARD. Ref Tmsfo to make an A.D.S. F.A.3.9 Fresne Sheet 62 N.E.	
	11.7.16		Admitted from 6 p.m.(10) - 6 A.M. 26 Off + 253. O.R. admitted from 6.6.2a. 6 p.m. 10 Off + 176. O.R. Germans 7	
	12.7.16		Admitted from 6 p.m.(11) - 6 A.M. 13 Off - 107 O.R. D.D.M.S XV Corps visited the Ambulance	
	13.7.16		Capt. C. J. O'REILLY proceeded with 2 sections & bearers to take over A.D.S. MAMETZ from the 23rd F.A. Capt. JARDINE returned from the ORCHARD to be A.D.S. MAMETZ leaving 1 Sec. & 8 men at the D.S. THE ORCHARD. The D.G. visited the Ambulance during the afternoon. At 6 p.m. all mules + Horse Ambulances/personnel of the D.C.S. at RECORDEL + horse mules returns of or. 22" F.A. Very quiet day only 2 O.R. Admitted from 6 A.M. - 6 P.M.	

WAR DIARY or INTELLIGENCE SUMMARY

No. 21 FIELD AMBULANCE

JULY 1916

Army Form C. 2118.

Place	Date	Hour	Summary of Events and Information	Remarks and references to Appendices
MORLANCOURT	14/7/16		The 20th 13th Coy moved to the attack at 3.25 a.m. First casualties arrived at 3.45 a.m. Admitted from 6 A.M (13) - 6 A.M. 1 Off + 6. O.R. Surg Genl MACPHERSON visited the Ambulance. Detained from 6 A.M - 6 P.M. 13 Off + 114. O.R	
	15/7/16		Admitted from 6 P.M (14th) - 6 A.M 20 Off + 158. O.R. D.M.S. 6th Corps visited the Ambulance. 6.2 P.M + D.S MANGETZ inspected clear. Admitted from 6 A.M to 6 P.M 14 Off 119. O.R + 3 Indians.	
	16/7/16		Admitted from 6 P.M (15th) to 6 A.M 11 Officers 109 O.R + 1 machine. Admitted from 6 A.M - 6 P.M 7 Officers - 68. O.R. Total A.D.S at MAMETZ at 5 P.M. no cases for evacuation.	
	17/7/16		Admitted from 6 A.M (16) - 6 A.M. 2 Officers + 9. O.R. Admitted from 6 A.M - 6 P.M 15 O.R.	
	18/7/16		Admitted from 6 P.M (17) 5. Off + 11. O.R. Received information from the 91st Bde - on forward The Bye will move tomorrow the 19th inst to area Nontride & WILLOW AVENUE STREAM. Between BECORDEL + MEAULTE about E.12.D. The Bde HQ's will be at E.12.c1.3. Admitted from 6.A.M - 6.p.M 1. Off + 16. O.R. Received orders from the 91st Bde that 7th Div. will attack at ZERO hour on the 19th inst. 6.30 P.M. Wire received. The Attack Tomorrow Tomorrow is postponed until further orders.	

WAR DIARY or INTELLIGENCE SUMMARY

Army Form C. 2118.

No 21 FIELD AMBULANCE

JULY 1916.

Place	Date	Hour	Summary of Events and Information	Remarks and references to Appendices
MORLANCOURT	19-7-16		Admitted from 6 p.m (18th) — 6 a.m. 3 O/R + 23. O.R. by 9 amb. Wagon conveyed admissions from G.A. Zoo to 6 p.m. 2 O.R.	TRENCH MAP 62 D NE
		7 p.m.	Received an order that the Div. would attack at 7.2.20 on the 20th inst.	
		9 p.m.	Received orders from A.D.M.S. that 21st F.A. Bearer Div. will relieve the 22nd F.A. at FLAT IRON Copse. A car horsing zone will be established at F.4.c in MAMETZ Wood. Arrangements made by O. 23.Z.12	
	20-7-16		Admitted from 6 p.m (19th) — 6 a.m. 4 Off. 7 O.R. The 20th B'ge attacked and took the attack sub-	
		3.30 a.m.	At 3.40 a.m. the first wounded arrived at the MAIN D.S. Casualties were not heavy	
			Transfer Ambulance from 6 a.m. 6 p.m. 12 Off + 88. O.R. At breakdown + evacuation of wounded the unit was very satisfactory. Received wounded from 21 DINIS. C & Ch. employed to remove our Main D.Stn. + A.D.S MAMETZ	
		10 p.m.	A.D.S MAMETZ taken over by the 13th F.A. Capt. O'REILLY & VARDINIS took the bearer Div. reformed HQ Bye nrd. 3 a.m. in the 2nd inst. During the fighting from the 1st inst. One Person was killed, one chiefly wounded + 11 slight received return.	
	21-7-16		Admitted from 6 p.m. (20th) — 6 a.m. 2 Off + 14.O.R. Received an order to proceed via MAIN D.Stn to O.C. 13th F.A. 3rd Div, on completion to proceed by rt. Ballom to HEILLY	
		1.30 p.m.	The Ambulance marched to HEILLY arriving at 3 p.m.	
		3.30 p.m.	Visited Biv—by— Correspondent that these have been prepared not also	
HEILLY	22-7-16		All sick on firing without to send direct to the field ambulance at MERICOURT	

WAR DIARY
or
INTELLIGENCE SUMMARY

Army Form C. 2118.

No 11 Field Ambulance July 1916

Place	Date	Hour	Summary of Events and Information	Remarks and references to Appendices
HEILLY	23.7.16 to 31.7.16		Ambulances still worked. All sick are being sent to 13' F.A. at DERNACOURT.	Ref Colonel Ingh 140,000

In the Field
31.7.16

A.J.Ingh lt
Mj R.A.M.C.
21st F A

No. 21. Field Ambulance.

COMMITTEE FOR THE
MEDICAL HISTORY OF THE WAR
Date 26 OCT 1915

Army Form C. 2118.

WAR DIARY
No 21 FIELD AMBULANCE

Vol. 20

INTELLIGENCE SUMMARY

(Erase heading not required.)

Place	Date	Hour	Summary of Events and Information	Remarks and references to Appendices
HEILLY	12/8/16		Nothing to note. The Ambulance was closed + resting.	
	13/8/16		Lt. T. Dowzer R.A.M.C. proceeded as M.O. I/c 2/8th Royal Irish Regt. Capt D. Marr R.A.M.C. Millan and B. Tool Sick Div. proceeded as XV Corps Mo. O.8th in Temp duty. Received instructions from the A.D.M.S. to move the Ambulance to RIBEMONT + form a Rt. Temp. ALBERT.	Rt. Temp. ALBERT 1/12 mm
RIBEMONT	14/8/16		G. Hospital. branched at 4 p.m. Arrived at RIBEMONT at 4.45 p.m. Hospital open at 6 p.m. Ready for reception of sick. A.D.M.S. visited team balance.	
	16/8/16		A.D.M.S. visited the Ambulance.	
	29/8/16		Lt. R. Barnes proceeded on temp duty as M.O.I/c 21st Manchesters in relief of J	
	21/8/16		Lt. Barrett who joined this Ambulance for duty.	
	23/8/16		Capt. J.R. McMillan was evacuated (sick) to 36 C.C.S. The A.D.M.S. visited the Team balance.	
	26/8/16		Lt. Joyce reported for duty from No 5 C.C.S.	
	27/8/16		A.D.M.S. visited the Ambulance.	

WAR DIARY or INTELLIGENCE SUMMARY

Army Form C. 2118.

No 2¹ Field Ambulance

Place	Date	Hour	Summary of Events and Information	Remarks and references to Appendices
RIDEMONT	28/8/16		Lt VOYCE proceeded on temp duty as M O/c 1st South Staffs	
	30/8/16		Lt BARRETT proceeded on temp duty as MO/c 1st R W F	
			Lt JOYCE rejoined from 1st S.S.	
	31/8/16		Received instructions from A.D.M.S to take over A.D.S. BERNAFAY WOOD from the 22nd F.A. Capt O'REILLY with two bearer sub divisions proceeded to FRICOURT. The Div Coll Stn + bearer divn from the right Will proceeds to take over the A D S in	ALBERT MAP 62.D.N.E at BERNAFAY
	1st Sept		Lt E.B BARNES rejoined from duty from the 21st MANCHESTERS	

J.M. Prested
2nd Sept 1916

W D Long L
Maj R.A.M.C
V
2/D F.A

7th Division

140/1/188

Sept 1915
Oct 1916
5

OB. 21 70. -

COMMITTEE FOR THE
MEDICAL HISTORY OF THE WAR
Date -2 DEC. 1915

Army Form C. 2118.

WAR DIARY
or
INTELLIGENCE SUMMARY

(Erase heading not required.)

No. 21 Field Ambulance

September 1916

Place	Date	Hour	Summary of Events and Information	Remarks and references to Appendices
RIDGEMONT	1/9/16		Capt O'REILLY took over the A.D.S at BERNAFAY WOOD from Lt 29th F.A. Capt J.F BROUGHTON posted to the A.D.S for duty. Lt JOYCE proceeded on temp: duty as M.O i/c 1st South Staffs. Lt BARNES rejoined for duty from the 2/1st MANCHESTERS.	Rt Troops ALBERT Cmd 1 wound
	3/9/16		Lt BARNES proceeded to the A.D.S BERNAFAY WOOD	
	2/9/16		Capt R.G BROWN joined for duty from N°.3 GENERAL HOSP. Lt BARNES posted as M. O/c 1st/1st N.F for period on rel: duty of Lt BARRETT. Lt BARRETT proceeded to the A.D.S.	
	5/9/16		Received instructions from the A.D.M.S. to take over charge of the XV CORPS REST Station at BECRE. Removed all my patients from BERNAFAY to CORPS REST Stn. II D.D.M.S XV CORPS visited the Hospital. Took over charge of CORPS REST Stn at BERNACOURT. D.D.M.S XV CORPS visited the Rest Stn.	
	6/9/16		A.D.M.S received 65 patients from CORPS REST Stn at BERNACOURT.	
	9/9/16		Lt JOYCE rejoined for duty from 1st South Staffs. Capt O'REILLY with A.D.S trans handed over the A.D.S BERNAFAY WOOD to N° 2/1st Field Amb. and rejoined Hd Qrs. Wessex	
DUIRE	10/9/16		Received instructions from D.D.M.S XV CORPS to hand over on the 12th inst. the CORPS REST Stn to N° 2nd 1st WEST LANCS Field Ambulance.	

Army Form C. 2118.

WAR DIARY
or
INTELLIGENCE SUMMARY   No. 21 Field Ambulance.

(Erase heading not required.)

September 1916

Place	Date	Hour	Summary of Events and Information	Remarks and references to Appendices
BUIRE	11/9/16		Surg. Gen O'KEEFE visited the CORPS Rest Stn.	
	12/9/16		Handed over the CORPS REST Stn to the 2/1st WEST LANCS Field Ambulance. Received instructions from the XV CORPS. As follows:- On the 13th inst:- the Ambulance will proceed to DOURS + bivouac for the night. On the 14th inst the unit will be continued to CROUY, on the 15th inst to the Hospital will be removed to Hôpital 5 - HUCHENVILLE.	
	13/9/16		Left BUIRE at 2 p.m. + marched to DOURS arriving at 5.30. Bivouacked just NORTH of DOURS for the night.	
DOURS	14/9/16		Left DOURS at 7.50 a.m. and marched via AMIENS to CROUY arriving about 4 p.m. 6 p.m. billetted for the night.	
CROUY	15/9/16		Left CROUY at 8.40 a.m. and marched to their new home at HUCHENVILLE arriving at 1.15 p.m.	
HUCHENVILLE	16/9/16		Received instructions from Capt. R.J. BROWN RAMC to proceed to No 3 GEN. Hosp. for duty. Capt. R.J. BROWN proceeded to No 3 GEN. HOSP. for duty. Received instructions from the A.D.M.S. to form a small Hosp. + to attend the sick from the 91st & 135th Brigades of the 77th Divl. A.D.M.S. visited the Ambulance & Convalescent & laid the Ambulances in readiness to receive patients. Lieut. Col BROWN R.A.M.C. & 77 Divl.	

Army Form C. 2118.

WAR DIARY
or
INTELLIGENCE SUMMARY   No. 21 Field Ambulance
(Erase heading not required.)

September 1916.

Place	Date	Hour	Summary of Events and Information	Remarks and references to Appendices
HUCHENNEVILLE	16/9/16		Received instructions from the ADMS for the Ambulance to entrain at ABBEVILLE on 17th inst. at 7.30 a.m. The Ambulance left at the entraining point at the hour before hour of departure.	
METEREN	18/9/16		Entrained at 3 a.m. to ABBEVILLE Stn. entrained at left ABBEVILLE at 4 p.m. detrained & marched to BAILLEUL at 4 p.m. arrived at METEREN arriving at 10 p.m.	
"	19/9/16		Received Instructions from the O.C. 1/1 NS-in-F Amb – On the 21st inst. the Bearer Subdivision A.D.S. at ESTAMINET. U.19.d.1.7 from the 59th F.A. on the 22nd inst. to take over the Dressing Stn. NIEPPE from the 59th F.A.	Ref: Trench map 33 SW
"	21/9/16		Capt. E.B. JARDINE + Lt. McKENZIE with the Bearer Sub-div took over at 6 U.19.d.1.7 + took over the A.D.S. from the 59th F.A.	
NIEPPE	22/9/16		Ambulance marched from METEREN at O.C. in Ammy at NIEPPE at 11 a.m. at 10 a.m. took over the Main Dressing Stn. NIEPPE from the 59th F.A.	Ref: Trench 28 SW + 36 NW
"	23/9/16		Capt. JARDINE proceeded on leave Capt. BROUGHTON proceeded to A.D.S. Lt. JOYCE proceed duty on temp duty as M.O/c 2/1st MANCHESTERS. Lt DOCKETT attended to Alarm of Ambulance at BAILLEUL in absence of above surgeons.	
"	24/9/16		The A.D.M.S. visited the Ambulance.	

Army Form C. 2118.

WAR DIARY
or
INTELLIGENCE SUMMARY

(Erase heading not required.)

N° 21 Field Ambulance

September 1916.

Place	Date	Hour	Summary of Events and Information	Remarks and references to Appendices
NIEPPE	26/9/16		Lt A Barrett proceeded to the 51st Div for duty.	
	27/9/16		D.D.M.S IX Corps visited the Ambulance.	
	30/9/16		G.O.C 7th Division visited the Ambulance.	

R. L. Boyd lt
Maj Munroe
OC 21st F.A.

3.10.16

Army Form C. 2118.

WAR DIARY
or
INTELLIGENCE SUMMARY
(Erase heading not required.)

Instructions regarding War Diaries and Intelligence Summaries are contained in F.S. Regs., Part II. and the Staff Manual respectively. Title Pages will be prepared in manuscript.

Place	Date	Hour	Summary of Events and Information	Remarks and references to Appendices
NIEPPE	3/10/16		Lt DOWZER proceeded on trans duty to M O/c 22" MANCHESTERS.	R. of trups formed 35 NM
"	5/10/16		Lt McKENZIE proceeded on temp duty to M O/c IX CORPS R.E. Capt D. MARR proceeded to the A.D.S for duty	
"	9/10/16		Capt E.B JARDINE returned from leave.	
"	10/10/16		Capt. D. MARR rejoined from the A.D.S. Capt JARDINE proceeded to the M.D.S Lt JOYCE rejoined for duty from the 21st MANCHESTERS. Capt O'REILLY proceeded on leave.	
"	15/10/16		Lt DOWZER rejoined for duty from the 22" MANCHESTERS. Lt McKENZIE rejoined for duty from the IX CORPS R.E. + proceeded to the A.D.S in relief of Capt BROUGHTON who rejoined H.Q 2nd.	
"	16/10/16		D.D.M.S IX CORPS visited the turn in camp.	
"	18/10/16		A.D.M.S visited the turn in camp.	

Army Form C. 2118.

WAR DIARY
or
INTELLIGENCE SUMMARY

21 2d Aust
Vol 22

(Erase heading not required.)

Instructions regarding War Diaries and Intelligence Summaries are contained in F. S. Regs., Part II. and the Staff Manual respectively. Title Pages will be prepared in manuscript.

Place	Date	Hour	Summary of Events and Information	Remarks and references to Appendices
NIEPPE	24/10/16		Lt T Dowzer proceeded on leave	REF MAP TRENCH 36 N.W.
B.16.C.6.6.	28/10/16		Lt McKenzie proceeded on temp duty to O/C 2' Queens	
	29/10/16		Capt D Marr proceeded to Lt. A.D.S. for duty Capt O Reilly returned from leave	
			Lt Joyce proceeded on leave	
	31/10/16		A.D.M.S. visited (B) Tm Palemon Received instructions to forward am A.D.S. to H.Q. 75 I Aberdeen Avenue on the 2nd Nov 1916.	

1/11/16.

[signature]
Lt Col R.O.C.
O.C. 21 C.F.A

140/849.

21st Field Ambulance

COMMITTEE FOR THE
MEDICAL HISTORY OF THE WAR
Date -3 JAN 1917

WAR DIARY or INTELLIGENCE SUMMARY

Army Form C. 2118.

21 2/A Amb
Vol 23

Place	Date	Hour	Summary of Events and Information	Remarks and references to Appendices
NIEPPE	1/10/16		Handed over A.D.S. col 4.19 D.1.7 to the 75th Field Ambulance.	Ref. French 1/20,000 NIEPPE
	2/10/16		Handed over the main Dress. ng Station at NIEPPE to the 75 F.A. Left NIEPPE at 10.4. pm and marched to LA CRECHE & billeted col for the nig ht.	
LA CRECHE	8/10/16		Marched from LA CRECHE to METERN. × 36 A 6.4.	
METERN	9/10/16	8.30 am	Left X36 A.6.4. and marched to STAPLE.	HAZEBROUCK 3 A. 1/100,000
STAPLE	10/10/16 10/10/16	8.15 am	Marched from STAPLE to ST. MARTIN. Capt. E.B.JARDINE RAMC assumed the military com.	
ST. MARTIN	11/10/16	10.30 am	Marched from ST. MARTIN to EPERLECQUES.	
EPERLECQUES	15/10/16	9.15 am	Marched from EPERLECQUES to PIHEM.	
PIHEM	16/10/16	9.30 am	Marched from PIHEM to CUHEM.	
CUHEM	18/10/16	9.30 am	Marched from CUHEM to TENEUR.	
TENEUR	19/10/16	10 am	Marched from TENEUR to FREVENT.	LENS Map Sheet 11 1/100,000
FREVENT	20/10/16	11 a.m.	Marched from FREVENT to NOEUX.	
BEAUVAL	21/10/16	9 a.m.	Marched from NOEUX to BEAUVAL.	
ACHEUX	22/10/16	9.45 am	Marched from BEAUVAL to ACHEUX.	

Army Form C. 2118.

WAR DIARY
or
INTELLIGENCE SUMMARY
(Erase heading not required.)

Place	Date	Hour	Summary of Events and Information	Remarks and references to Appendices
ACHEUX	23/11/16	3.30 PM	Travelled from ACHEUX to FORCEVILLE. Received instructions from the A.D.M.S to take over the Main Dressing Station at FORCEVILLE & the A.D.S. at MAILLY-MAILLET and Acc Hanvillers	See LENS maps No 11 1:100,000
FORCEVILLE			from the 2nd/1st Highland Field Amb. CAPT O'REILLY & LT JOYCE with A+B teams proceed to the A.D.S. to take over. Main Dressing Station taken over by 6 p.m.	"
"	25/11/16		Received instructions from the A.D.M.S to take over the V Corps Rest Station at CLAIRFAYE from the 50th F.A. CAPT BROUGHTON proceeded with an Advanced party to Rest Station.	
CLAIRFAYE	26/11/16		Took over V Corps Rest Sta from the 50th F.A. 580 patients taken over.	
"	28/11/16		D.D.M.S V Corps visited the Rest Stn	
"	29/11/16		D.M.S V Army visited the Rest Sta.	

R J Gray lt
Lt&stM.R.P.C
O C 2/1st F.A.

In the Field
1.12.16

140/1900.

21st Field Ambulance.

COMMITTEE FOR THE
MEDICAL HISTORY OF THE WAR
Date 31 JAN. 1917

Army Form C. 2118.

WAR DIARY
or
INTELLIGENCE SUMMARY
(Erase heading not required.)

Vol 2 | Remarks and references to Appendices: LENS MAP 71011. 1/100,000

Place	Date	Hour	Summary of Events and Information	Remarks
CLAIRFAYE	4/12/16		A.D.M.S. visited the Regt. Stn. & gave instructions to close the stn. down & to transfer all sick and stretcher cases to the 7th Div. Relgn. Stn. at ACHEUX.	
	6/12/16		Received instructions from the O.O. i/c to move the H.Q. of the Ambulance to MAILLEY MAILLET & was given a hoisting party at CLAIRFAYE.	
		2.30pm	H.Q. to move from CLAIRFAYE to MAILLEY MAILLET. Capt. MARR took over charge of Regt. Stn. Lt. T. DOWZER proceeded as M.O.i/c 22nd Inniskillins in place of Capt. McGREGOR (wounded).	
MAILLEY MAILLET	7/12/16		Lt. McKENZIE proceeded as M.O.i/c 1st South Staffs in place of Capt. REYNOLDS (evacuated sick).	
	10/12/16		A.D.M.S. visited the Amb. balance.	
	13/12/16		Lt. C.R. ROYCE proceeded to England on 10 days leave on termn. of his contract. Lt. & QM J. GRIGGS proceeded on leave.	
	15/12/16		Received instructions from the A.D.M.S. to hand over the Coys. Roel Stn. at CLAIRFAYE to the 34th F.A. & to move the transport to BERTRANCOURT.	
	17/12/16		Handed Regt. Stn. over to the 34th F.A. & moved the transport to BERTRANCOURT.	
	18/12/16		A.D.M.S. visited the Amb. balance.	

WAR DIARY
or
INTELLIGENCE SUMMARY

(Erase heading not required.)

Army Form C. 2118.

Place	Date	Hour	Summary of Events and Information	Remarks and references to Appendices
MALLEY MALLET	24/12/16		Capt. J. F. Broughton proceeded on leave.	LENS MAP Sh 11. 1.100,000
"	25/12/16		Capt. N. P. PRITCHARD joined for duty from No 3 C.C.S.	
"	30/12/16		A.D.M.S. visited the ambulance.	

1/1/17.

J. F. Long? Lt Col Ml RAMC
O 2/1st F.A.

Jan 1917

7th Div.

No. 21. Field Ambulance

140/1917.

COMMITTEE FOR THE
MEDICAL HISTORY OF THE WAR
Date   13 MAR. 1917

Army Form C. 2118.

WAR DIARY
or
INTELLIGENCE SUMMARY
(Erase heading not required.)

21 Fd Amb Vol 25

Place	Date	Hour	Summary of Events and Information	Remarks and references to Appendices
MAILLY	4/1/17		A.D.M.S. visited the Ambulance.	LENS MAP VII. II.D.N.W.
MAILLY	5/1/17		CAPT. V.F. BROUGHTON proceeded on temp duty to M.O.i/c 252 Coy R.E.	
	6/1/17		CAPT. PRITCHARD proceeded on temp duty as M.O.i/c 2nd BORDER Regt.	
"	10/1/17		CAPT JARDINE proceeded to WHITE CITY & took over charge of 91st A.D.S.	
"	11/1/17	6.20 p.m.	The 91st Inf Bde attacked and captured MUNICH TRENCH.	
"		8.30 p.m.	The Field Amb. J men in rest arrived. By 9 p.m. all stretcher first line collection posts were open. By 11 p.m. about 200 stretcher cases had come down the A.D.S. and R.A.P. bearer Divns. Two bearer divns are staying by arrangement at Coy VARDINE Officer i/c A.D.S.	
"	12/1/17	10 AM	Around half bearer staff from the M.D.S.	
"	17/1/17		Received instructions from the V Corps A.D.M.S. to transfer over the evacuation of the Corps Main Dressing Stn to the 37th F.A. Handed over the V CORPS M.D.S to the 37 F.A.	
"	19/1/17		Received instructions from the A.D.M.S. V Corps to transfer over the Front D.S. & the 91st F.A. on the 20th inst, and to transfer over the A.D.S. at WHITE CITY on the 20th inst to the 23rd F.A. To be ready to Transfer over the 91st & 96th Bde's Other on the 21st inst.	

Army Form C. 2118.

WAR DIARY
or
INTELLIGENCE SUMMARY
(Erase heading not required.)

Instructions regarding War Diaries and Intelligence Summaries are contained in F. S. Regs., Part II. and the Staff Manual respectively. Title Pages will be prepared in manuscript.

Place	Date	Hour	Summary of Events and Information	Remarks and references to Appendices
MAILLEY	20/1/17		Handed over the A.D.S. at WHITE CITY to the 23rd F.A. and marched over that	Ref: map RENS sheet 11 1/100,000
MAILLET	21/1/17		M.D.S. Lts 91st F.A. Received instructions from the 91st Inf. Bde. to march at 10.30 a.m. on the 21st inst. to VAL de MAISON.	
	21/1/17		Capt. PRITCHARD rejoined for duty from the 2nd Border Regt. Marched at 10.30 a.m. and arrived at VAL de MAISON at 4 p.m.	
VAL-de-MAISON	22/1/17		Capt. G.R. MACKAY reported for duty from No 5 Rest Camp Boulogne	
	23/1/17		Capt. PRITCHARD proceeded on temp. duty as M.O. 1st S. Staffs Regt. The following men were awarded the Military Medal. No 19187 Pte C.V. HUNT No 4367 Pte R. HOCKHEIMER 7932 Pte G/PyC A.R. GILBERSTON.	
	24/1/17		The following NCOs & men were mentioned (un instruct.) the Military field 19206 Cpl C. SPEELER D.C.M. No 5137 Pte BLACKWELL A. No 230 JC Pte J. McCulloch	
	25/1/17		Capt. T. BROUGHTON rejoined from the 25th Roy. R.P.	
	26/1/17		A.+ 8 XIV Corps marched thro' the Ambulance. Brig. General 22/37/Bde.43 directed the Ambulance	
	28/1/17		67. O.R. marched on temp. duty to No 2 C.C.S. VARENNES	

Army Form C. 2118.

WAR DIARY or INTELLIGENCE SUMMARY
(Erase heading not required.)

Place	Date	Hour	Summary of Events and Information	Remarks and references to Appendices
VAL-cl-MAISON	29/1/17		D.D.M.S XIIII Corps visited this am re billeting	Insp. Ref. £ =NSIWII 1.1.07000
	29/1/17		Capt MACKAY proceeded on temp/y duty to M.O./c 1st R.W.F	

H J Brig /c
Lieut. Col. R.A.M.C
OC 21ᵘᵗ F.A.

1ˢᵗ Feb 1917.

140/1994.

1.Div.

No. 21. Field Ambulance.

Army Form C. 2118.

WAR DIARY
or
INTELLIGENCE SUMMARY

(Erase heading not required.)

Vol 26

Place	Date	Hour	Summary of Events and Information	Remarks and references to Appendices
VAL de MAISON	2/2/17		Capt Broughton proceeded on temp duty as M.O i/c 22nd Manchester Regt.	R&F LENS MAR/1917
			Capt D. Marr proceeded on leave.	MAR/1917
	3/2/17		Capt A.E. Roberts joined for duty from No 14 Gen. Hosp.	
"	6/2/17		Capt Roberts proceeded on temp duty as M.O i/c 7th D.A.C.	
"	7/2/17		Capt Mackay rejoined from 1st R.W.F.	
"	8/2/17		Capt Mackay proceeded on temp duty as M.O i/c 7th Div. R.E.	
"	9/2/17		Capt Pritchard rejoined from 1st S. Staffs Regt.	
"	13/2/17		G.O.C. VII Div visited the Ambulance.	
"	14/2/17		A.D.M.S. inspected B Section. Barracks. Personnel overhaul of the Ambulance.	
"	15/2/17		A.D.M.S. visited the Ambulance. Capt F.B Jardine proceeded on temp duty as M.O i/c 20th Manchester. Capt N. Pritchard R.A.M.C. proceeded on 96 hours leave to Paris.	

WAR DIARY
or
INTELLIGENCE SUMMARY

Army Form C. 2118.

Place	Date	Hour	Summary of Events and Information	Remarks and references to Appendices
VAL DE MAISON	17/2/17		Divisional Sports in honour of General Neville. 30 men and 2 ambulance wagons attended. O/C Capt. D.M. Farr R.A.M.C.	
	19/2/17		B section under Capt. O'Reilly MacInnes handed over Received by Capt. Carpenter. Lieut. A. Ball and T. Stanly R.A.M.C joined from 23rd Field Ambulance for temporary duty with this unit.	
	20/2/17		D.A.D.M.S. visited the Unit. Capt. N.P. Pritchard returned from leave Received orders from A.D.M.S. to move to Corps Rest Station Vauchelles on 22nd inst. Capt. N.P. Pritchard R.A.M.C took on medical charge	
	21/2/17		Capt. Pardine rejoined his unit of 20th Manchester Regt.	
VAUCHELLES	22/2/17	-	Moved the ambulance from Val de Maison to V/a Corps Rest Sta Vauchelles under orders of A.D.M.S. Arrived at Vauchelles 4-30 P.M.	
	23/2/17		Under orders of A.D.M.S. Lieuts. Stanly and Ball rejoined 23rd Field Ambulance. The party of 67 O.R. upward from duty cut no 47 C.C.S. VARENNES.	
	24/2/17		Lt. Werlan left on 2 days leave this morning at A.M. Capt. J.F. Broughton rejoined from duty with 22nd Manchester Regt.	

Army Form C. 2118.

WAR DIARY
or
INTELLIGENCE SUMMARY
(Erase heading not required.)

21st FIELD AMBULANCE
Date FEBRUARY
7th DIVISION

Place	Date	Hour	Summary of Events and Information	Remarks and references to Appendices
VAUCHELLES	26/2/17		Capt. R.G.R. MACKAY. RAMC. rejoined from duty with 7th Divn R.E.	
"	27/2/17		ADMS. visited the unit – Capt. G.R. MACKAY proceeded in temporary charge of 12th West Riding Labour Battn. DADMS. v Capts v unts 21st ambulance.	
"	28/2/17		Capt. J.C. Buxton R.A.M.C. joined for duty from 7th Div R.E.	

F.W. Warren
Capt. RAMC
for O.C. 21 Field Ambulance

Marian S

7th Dn

No. 21. Field Ambulance.

14/204

COMMITTEE FOR THE
MEDICAL HISTORY OF THE WAR
Date 11 MAY 1917

Army Form C. 2118.

WAR DIARY
or
INTELLIGENCE SUMMARY
(Erase heading not required.)

Instructions regarding War Diaries and Intelligence Summaries are contained in F. S. Regs., Part II. and the Staff Manual respectively. Title Pages will be prepared in manuscript.

Place	Date	Hour	Summary of Events and Information	Remarks and references to Appendices
MUNCHELLES	1/3/17		Capts. G.P. Kidd and A.W. Young R.A.M.C. with 13 O.R. joined for duty from 59th Fd. Amb. – Lt. Col. Heelan returned from 2 days leave.	MAP 12-17 LENS Nos 11, 1/5R,000
"	2/3/17		D.A.D.M.S. 7th Div. visited Ambulance – Lt. Col. N.G. WRIGHT D.S.O. R.A.M.C. O.C. this unit, returned from leave.	
"	3/3/17		Capt. A.F. READDIE joined for duty from M.O i/c 20 MANCH ESTERS.	
"	4/3/17		A.D.M.S. visited the Units. Rest Stn. ready to receive 200 patients. D.M. V Corps visited the Am. internal.	
"	6/3/17		Capt. T.C. BURTON R.A.M.C. proceeded on M.O. i/c 46th RESERVE PARK.	
"	7/3/17		Capt. E.V. CLARKE joined for duty from M.O i/c 46th RESERVE PARK.	
"	8/3/17		Capt. G.P. KIDD & A.W. YOUNG R.A.M.C. 57th F.A. rejoined their unit.	
"	11/3/17		Q.M.S. Coffs visited the Rest Stn.	
"	13/3/17		Capt. E.B. JARDINE + CLARKE proceeded with Div. to MAILLY MAILLET.	

Army Form C. 2118.

WAR DIARY
or
INTELLIGENCE SUMMARY
(Erase heading not required.)

Instructions regarding War Diaries and Intelligence Summaries are contained in F. S. Regs., Part II. and the Staff Manual respectively. Title Pages will be prepared in manuscript.

Place	Date	Hour	Summary of Events and Information	Remarks and references to Appendices
VAUCHELLES	16/3/17		D.M.S V Corps visited the Rest Stn	Mch Ref LENS Sh 11 1/100,000
	17/3/17		Capt MACKAY reported for duty from In O/c 12 Cdn Fd Amb West Yorks. Received instructions from the N.D.M.S to transport over the V Corps Rest Station to the 2nd North Mid Ambulance also to transport from 1st N.M.S.B. based at BERTRANCOURT Received no instructions from 1st N.M.S.B. based at BERTRANCOURT	
BERTRANCOURT	21/3/17		Sent to take over the site occupied by the 23rd F.A. Transfer from VAUCHELLES at 10 A.M. arrived at BERTRANCOURT 3.45 P.M.	
	24/3/17		Received instructions from the A.D.M.S to take over on the 25th inst the Dressing Station – RED HOUSE MAILLY MAILLET and the V Corps Rest Stn R.19 central from the 23rd F.A. Capt MACKAY forwarded temp attd as M.O/c 1/5th MANCHESTERS.	
MAILLY MAILLET RED HOUSE	25/3/17		Took over Dressing Stn "RED HOUSE" MAILLY MAILLET and Rest Stn at R.19. central from the 23rd F.A. Capt D. MARR and READDIE proceeded at BERTRANCO to take Full LENS O/N	

21st FIELD AMBULANCE
Date MARCH 1917.
7th DIVISION

WAR DIARY or INTELLIGENCE SUMMARY

Army Form C. 2118.

[Stamp: 21st FIELD AMBULANCE, Date MARCH 1917, 7th DIVISION]

Place	Date	Hour	Summary of Events and Information	Remarks and references to Appendices
MAILLY-MAILLET (RED HOUSE)	28/3/17		Took over charge of this of communication of sick from Puisieux-au-Mont from the 23rd F.A. Capt. JARDINE with 20 bearers took charge & of running station at Puisieux, also took over the 22 2LR 3rd F.A's are attached to these Amb. for that purpose.	
	29/3/17		Attached advance post at Skunk Post & SERRE.	
	29/3/17		A.D.M.S visited the Amb.	
	30/3/17		D.D.M.S V Corps visited the Amb. also.	
	31/3/17		Capt. READ D[?] was evacuated to No. 29½ South Midland C.C.S suffering from Trench Fever.	

[Signature]
Lt Col R.A.M.C
O.C 21st F.A.
2nd April 1917.

140/2086

COMMITTEE FOR THE
MEDICAL HISTORY OF THE WAR
Date −6 JUN. 1917

April 1917

S

7th Divn.

No 21. F.A.

WAR DIARY
or
INTELLIGENCE SUMMARY

(Erase heading not required.)

Army Form C. 2118.

Place	Date	Hour	Summary of Events and Information	Remarks and references to Appendices
RED HOUSE MAILLY-MAILLET	3/4/17		Brown Oliver on the command Capt JARDINE forwarded from PLUISIEUX to ERNVILLERS and reported to OC 23rd F.A. for duty. Capt O'Reilly proceeded to PLUISIEUX in command of front line party.	FRANCE Sheet 57.D
"	4/4/17		Capt CLAUDE proceeded in temp. chg. of Lt 44 CCS	
"	5/4/17		Brown division proceeded from ERNVILLERS to PLUISIEUX. Capt O'Reilly rejoined HQ. Received instructions from the ADMS to close post at PLUISIEUX. When a Fd Amb takes over from the 63rd Div move to BERTRANCOURT to hand over the Fd Amb site to them & to withdraw the station HQ 20 AD 20 & men from RED House to P	
	6/4/17		17.6.7.3 and take over the 7th Div Rst Stn from the 23 CFA. Capt O'Reilly proceeded on tempy duty to the CCS	
	7/4/17		Handed over D Amb site at BERTRANCOURT to the 2/1 Home Counties F.A. Capt MARR & YOUNG with O section joined H.Q. Moved Fd Op from RED House MAILLY MAILLET to P 17.6.7.3 Capt JARDINE with rear chains rejoined H.Q. from PLUISIEUX	
	8/4/17		Handed over RED House site to 2/1 Home Counties F.A.	

WAR DIARY or INTELLIGENCE SUMMARY

Army Form C. 2118.

Place	Date	Hour	Summary of Events and Information	Remarks and references to Appendices
P.17.C.7.3	7/4/17		Moved HQrs from Red House Mailly Maillet to P.17.C.7.3 and took over charge	FRANCE 57.D
"	8/4/17		of Divisional Rest Stn from Capt Mackie 23rd F.A. Capt Mackie and section from the 20 S.F.A. rejoined their HQ 2. d. al Beuquoy.	
	9/4/17		Received instructions from A.D.M.S. to close down the Rest Stn + to remove all the patients who could not be fit for duty in 48 hours, and warm any patients to move that the HQ to Beuquoy and remain closed.	
	10/4/17		All patients either evacuated to a CCS on discharged to duty. Rest Station closed. Instructions from the A.D.M.S. to handover the Rest Station to a Field Amb of the 58th Div on the 11th inst. Capt F.B. Jardine with A + B Sections and Civilians proceeded to Beuquoy.	
	9/4/17		and were attached to the 23rd F.A.	
	11/4/17		Handed over Rest Stn to 2/3 Home Counties F.A. at 1.30 p.m. without incident moved at F.28.D.w. and remained closed.	
Beuquoy F.28.s.s.A. (57.D)	15/4/17		Received instructions from the G.O. + S. to takeover one officer + one clerk to proceed to the L'ABBAYE MORY to report to a/c 23rd F.A. Capt J.E. Broughton proceeded on this duty.	Short. 57.C.
	16/4/17		Capt D. Marr proceeded with C. Section to Ervillers to arrive at he Domny Stn and report with the A.D.M.S. 62nd Div	Short 57.C.

Army Form C. 2118.

WAR DIARY
or
INTELLIGENCE SUMMARY
(Erase heading not required.)

Instructions regarding War Diaries and Intelligence Summaries are contained in F. S. Regs., Part II. and the Staff Manual respectively. Title Pages will be prepared in manuscript.

Place	Date	Hour	Summary of Events and Information	Remarks and references to Appendices
Becquoy 728.56. A. (57.D)	16/4/17		Capt. Young - R.M. proceeded on temp. duty as M.O. %c 8th Devons.	Frame Sheet 57.D
	20/4/17		Capt. Mackay rejoined from temp. duty with the 21st Manchesters.	
	27/4/17		Capt. Readdie rejoined for duty from the 128 Scots Division via the Amb. via VII Division via the Amb.	
	22/4/17		Capt. F.B. Jardine proceeded on leave.	
	26/4/17		Capt. W.B. Tebson joined for duty from No 1 General Hospital Carwill Scott. Joined for duty from Tusteer Convalescent ch. 4.17.	
	30/4/17		A.D.M.S. visited the Ambulance.	

1st May 1917.

R J Long
Lt Col MC
O.C. 21st Field Ambulance

COMMITTEE FOR THE
MEDICAL HISTORY OF THE WAR
Date 10 JUL. 1917

No. 21. 7.a.

2nd Div

May 1917

WAR DIARY or INTELLIGENCE SUMMARY

Army Form C. 2118.

Place	Date	Hour	Summary of Events and Information	Remarks and references to Appendices
Bucquoy 7.2B.A.5.5.	2/5/17		Received instructions from the R.O.M.S. for two bearer Sub divisions to proceed at dawn tomorrow to MORY and come under orders of the O.C. Main D.R.S/7.	Ref. Map 57.C.
	3/5/17	3:30 a.m.	Capt. O'REILLY & MACKAY with two bearer Sub divisions marched to MORY.	
	6/5/17		Capt. E. B. JARDINE rejoined from leave. Received instructions from the A.D.M.S. to establish an Advanced Dressing Station in the neighbourhood of C.3.c.0.6 and relay from there the wounded. Went round from C.2.d central to BULLECOURT; the line I recommend I.B.4 by the L'écoust Succraine Road to Maine D.R. Sta. MORY. Established an Advanced Dressing Station at C.2.d.10.3. And a relay post at C.3.d.3.4.	
	7/5/17		Line of Sub divisions was to follows, for stretcher & walking wounded. R.A.P. 20th Inf/13 Sbde. R.A.P. stretcher wound U.28.C.3.3. Relay post C.3.d.3.4. A.D.S. C.2.d.10.3. Relay post on Ecoust Sucresis Road. C.B.A.2.4 from here the motor Ambulances evacuated all cases to the Main D.R. Sta. 21 ABBAYE MORY. Received instructions from the A.D.M.S. to take over Charge of the Main Dressing Sta. MORY from the 23rd F.A. Took over charge of the Main Dressing Station. MORY from the 23 F.A.	Troops Regt. D.V.D. 24 1/20,000
21 Main D.S. MORY.			Capt. JARDINE transferred to A.D.S. C.2.d.10.3.	

Army Form C. 2118.

WAR DIARY
or
INTELLIGENCE SUMMARY
(Erase heading not required.)

Instructions regarding War Diaries and Intelligence Summaries are contained in F.S. Regs., Part II. and the Staff Manual respectively. Title Pages will be prepared in manuscript.

Place	Date	Hour	Summary of Events and Information	Remarks and references to Appendices
LA-BOAYE NORY	8.5.17		Capt. CARR HARRIS, R.A.M.C. joined at BUGUOY for duty from the 4th C.C.S. Capt. MACKAY proceeded to ECOUST and took over charge of 17th F.A. O.S. from the 23rd F.A. Capt. BROUGHTON proceeded on leave.	Command Troops. 1.20. mm. O.31. D.24
	9.5.17		Owing to shell fire moved the M.D.S. from O.2. d. 10.3 to the valley at C.9. a.2.6. Wire & retrenchment in before.	
	10.5.17		Capt. JERSON proceeded to the 8th DEVONS in relief of Capt. YOUNG who on being relieved joined the 22nd F.A. for duty. D.A.M.S. VII Corps + A.D.M.S. VIIth Div. visited the Advanced Dressing Stn. 703305 Pte. Roy was killed in action and buried at NORY.	
	11.5.17	11.P.M.	The 2nd Queens reported several wounded lying out in BULLECOURT (doubtful) with 100 teams to try and collect them, only two Stretcher cases could be found, as all were found were already collected. Horse drawn were used for these stretcher squads.	
	12.5.17		Capt. JARDINE joined from the A.D.S. (VALLEY ROAD) to try relieved by LT. CLARKE. A.M. I.O. Officer of the 5th Div. Received two runners from the 2 A.M.S. to School. The village of the Main Dressing Stn. at NORY to Off. 2/2. H.C. F.A. S.O.(1)er. handing over the Camp School & fresh on the 15th inst.	

Army Form C. 2118.

WAR DIARY
or
INTELLIGENCE SUMMARY
(Erase heading not required.)

Instructions regarding War Diaries and Intelligence Summaries are contained in F. S. Regs., Part II. and the Staff Manual respectively. Title Pages will be prepared in manuscript.

Place	Date	Hour	Summary of Events and Information	Remarks and references to Appendices
2/1 A.G. & 7/2 Mory.	14/5/17		From instructions received from Mr. A.D.M.S. Capt Carr-Harris proceeded for duty with 1st Anzac Corps + Capt Clarke to 11th Div. Capt Renddis proceeded to the A.G.S. in temp. charge in relief of Capt. Clarke.	
	15/5/17		Handed over the Train D.2 Sh. at Mory to O.C. 2/2 H.C. F.A. and returned to Bucquoy.	
Bucquoy	16/5/17		Received instructions from the A.D.M.S. to take over field ambulance site at Bucquoy from the 2/2 West Riding F.A.	
			Took over from the 2/3 West Riding F.A. Capt. Mackay and Kerans were relief at Valley Post – G.R. a.2.6 relief by the 62nd Div. Capt O'Reilly and Kerans have relief at Valley Post – G.R. a.2.6 by the 3rd Div.	Mory Ref 57.G
	17/5/17		Capt. O'Reilly + Mackay and Kerans obtain leave reported H.Q. Stf.	
	20/5/17		Capt. F.B. Jardine proceeded on temp duty to M.O/c 23 H.A.G.	
	21/5/17		A.D.M.S. visited the Amb. Lines.	
	22/4/17		O.C. VII Div Train inspected the transport.	
	26/5/17		Capt. F. Mackay from the M.O. in temp. charge on tar O/c 2nd Warwicks	

2449 Wt. W14957/Mgo 750,000 1/16 J.B.C. & A. Forms/C.2118/12.

WAR DIARY or INTELLIGENCE SUMMARY

Army Form C. 2118.

Place	Date	Hour	Summary of Events and Information	Remarks and references to Appendices
Bucquoy	26/5/17		Capt T.F. Broughton returned from leave.	Msg Ref
			No 8404 Pte J Parkinson + No 9428 Pte PM. Harbottle have been awarded the Military Medal.	5.T.C.
	28/5/17		Capt Broughton proceeded on duty to the 8th Devons as 2nd i/c. Capt SF-p Huon rejoined from the 8 Devons.	

1st June 1917.

J. J. Broughton
Lt Col
Commanding 2nd Bn Royal Irish

140/230

No. 21. F.A.

COMMITTEE FOR THE
MEDICAL HISTORY OF THE WAR
Date -7 AUG.1917

Army Form C. 2118.

WAR DIARY
or
INTELLIGENCE SUMMARY
(Erase heading not required.)

Instructions regarding War Diaries and Intelligence Summaries are contained in F.S. Regs., Part II. and the Staff Manual respectively. Title Pages will be prepared in manuscript.

[Stamp: 21ST FIELD AMBULANCE * JUNE 1917 * 7th DIVISION]

Place	Date	Hour	Summary of Events and Information	Remarks and references to Appendices
Bucquoy	2/6/17		Capt JEPSON proceeded on leave. Capt B.M. Young joined for duty from the 35th Bde RFA	Trench Map 57c. 1:40,000
"	6/6/17		Capt JARDINE rejoined for duty from the 23rd H.A.G.	
"	8/6/17		Capt O'REILLY proceeded on leave.	
"	14/6/17		Capt B.M. Young proceeded as M.O i/c 35th Bde R.F.A in place of Capt L.D HARDIE. Capt HARDIE joined for duty.	
"	20/6/17		D.D.M.S V Corps visited the three Field Amb.	
"	22/6/17		Capt JEPSON proceeded on tour to study the M.O i/c 9th Division. Received instructions from the A.D.M.S to move the Ambulance on the 23rd inst. 2 to ERVILLERS taking over the Ambulance site from the 2/2 H.C. Field Ambulance, and to hand over the Ambulance site at Bucquoy to the 2/2 H.C. F.A.	
	23/6/17		Handed over site at Bucquoy to the 2/2 H.C. F.A. Marched out 10.45am to ERVILLERS & took over site from the 2/2 H.C. F.A. The Ambulance marched closed.	
ERVILLERS				

Army Form C. 2118.

WAR DIARY
or
INTELLIGENCE SUMMARY
(Erase heading not required.)

Instructions regarding War Diaries and Intelligence Summaries are contained in F.S. Regs., Part II. and the Staff Manual respectively. Title Pages will be prepared in manuscript.

21ST FIELD AMBULANCE
Date JUNE 1917
7th DIVISION

Place	Date	Hour	Summary of Events and Information	Remarks and references to Appendices
ERVILLERS	24/6/17		Capt. MACKAY proceeded on leave. A.D.M.S. visited the Amb.	Trips Ref 57.D.
	25/6/17		Capt. D. HARDIE proceeded on temp duty as M.O. to 1/5 Staffords.	
	26/6/17		Received instructions from the D.D.M.S. to proceed to BEHAGNIES on the 27th and find take over the Field Ambulance site from the 2/2 West Riding Field Ambulance.	
	27/6/17	7. a.m.	Left ERVILLERS and proceeded to BEHAGNIES and took over from the 2/2 W.R. Field Ambulance.	
BEHAGNIES	28/6/17		Capt. E.B. JARDINE was transferred sick to No. V Casualty Rest Station.	
	29/6/17		Capts. READDIE & SCOTT-BILL. A tent sub division rejoined from the C.C.S.	
	30/6/17		A.D.M.S. visited the Ambulance.	

B.P. Boyle
Lt. Col. R.A.M.C.
21st F.A.
1/7/17

140/293

COMMITTEE FOR THE
MEDICAL HISTORY OF THE WAR
Date   10 SEP. 1917

No. 21. 7. O.

Army Form C. 2118.

WAR DIARY
or
INTELLIGENCE SUMMARY
(Erase heading not required.)

Place	Date	Hour	Summary of Events and Information	Remarks and references to Appendices
BEHAGNIES	3/7/17		D.D.M.S. V Corps visited the Ambulance. A.D.M.S. visited the Ambulance.	Ref Traces 57.D. 1/40,000.
	5/7/17		Lt. P.M. T. GRIGGS proceeded on leave. Capt D. O'Reilly W/no attended 3 attd. sick leave from the 21.6.17 to the 13.7.17.	
"	7/7/17		Capt. MACKAY returned from leave.	
"	9/7/17		Capt. Scott posted med. as Tr.O to 1st South Staffords in relief of Capt. D. HARDIE. Capt. D. HARDIE rejoined CH Fd.	
"	15/7/17		Capt. C.J. O'REILLY rejoined from sick leave.	
"	17/7/17		Capt. E.B JARDINE was attached from the H.Q. C.C.S to the leave (sick). Lt. P.M. T. GRIGGS rejoined from leave.	
	22/7/17		Lt Col W. G WRIGHT - D.S.O., R.A.M.C commanding this Tuit proceeded on 14 days leave.	

WAR DIARY
or
INTELLIGENCE SUMMARY

Army Form C. 2118.

Place	Date	Hour	Summary of Events and Information	Remarks and references to Appendices
BRIMEULES	23-7-17		A.D.M.S. visited this ambulance	
	25-7-17		Capt D. HARDIE M.C. R.A.M.C and a Lieut and driver proceeded to No 3 Canadian Stationary Hosp Doullens for duty. Capt V.H.L. MacBurney R.A.M.C. joined for duty from VI Corps Depot Camp.	
	26-7-17		A.D.M.S. visited this ambulance — Capt W.H.L Macenery R.A.M.C. proceeded to 2nd Bn. H.A.C. for duty as M.O. in relief of Lt. A.H. POLLOCK R.A.M.C. sick.	
	28-7-17		Capt K.B. AIKMAN R.A.M.C joined for duty from 35 General Hospital	
	29-7-17		Capt K.B. AIKMAN R.A.M.C proceeded to report in duty to D.M.S. 4th Army	
	30-7-17		DADMS 7th Div visited the unit.	

B W Mann
Capt. R.A.M.C
for O.C. 21 F. Ambulance

140/2364

No. 21. 7.a.

COMMITTEE FOR THE
MEDICAL HISTORY OF THE WAR
Date -1 OCT.1917

Aug. 1917

Army Form C. 2118.

WAR DIARY
or
INTELLIGENCE SUMMARY
(Erase heading not required.)

[Stamp: 21st FIELD AMBULANCE, Date AUGUST 1917, 7th DIVISION]

Vol 3 2

Place	Date	Hour	Summary of Events and Information	Remarks and references to Appendices
BEHAGNIES	3/8/17		Returned from leave.	
"	6/8/17		Capt. F.S. CARSON from leave for duty from No.10 Can. Sect.	
"	7/8/17		Received instructions from the 91st Inf. Bde. to move 1st man balance on 1st 9th inst. to BIENVILLERS-au-Bois	
"	9/8/17		Marched from BEHAGNIES to BIENVILLERS-au-Bois arriving at 2.5.19. Left a watering party of N.CO.'s + men behind to guard the hutted camp site at BEHAGNIES.	LEWIS-Chab. 11. horses
BIENVILLERS au Bois	11/8/17		Capt. D. MARR + A.F. READ Die proceeded on leave. Capt. CARSON proceeded on temp. duty as M.O. to 35th Bde. R.F.A	
"	13/8/17		Received instructions from the M.D. F.A.s for Capt. D. HARDIE to proceed for duty to the 42nd Division.	
"	17/8/17		Capt. MacKAY posted here on temp. duty to No. 3 Canadian Hops.	
"	19/8/17		Capt. D. HARDIE proceeded for duty to the 42nd Division.	
"	23/8/17		Capt. BENSON posted for duty from the 62nd Division. Capt. A.F. READDIE returned from leave.	

Army Form C. 2118.

WAR DIARY
or
INTELLIGENCE SUMMARY

(Erase heading not required.)

21st FIELD AMBULANCE — AUGUST 1917 — 7th DIVISION

Instructions regarding War Diaries and Intelligence Summaries are contained in F. S. Regs., Part II. and the Staff Manual respectively. Title Pages will be prepared in manuscript.

Place	Date	Hour	Summary of Events and Information	Remarks and references to Appendices
BIENVILLERS au BOIS	28/8/17		Capt. A.F. READD proceeded on temp duty to MDS 2/4th MANCHESTERS. Capt. F.S. LARSON returned from the 3rd Belgn R.F.A. Capt. D.M. MARR returned from leave.	LENS Sheet No. 11.
"	29/8/17		Capt. V.M. BENIAN proceeded on temp duty to the 62nd Division. Capt. F.S. LARSON proceeded on temp duty to MD 1/2 2nd H.A.C.	
POMMERA	29/8/17		Left BIENVILLERS au Bois and marched to POMMERA. Lieut J.R. WILLIAMS R.A.M.C. RC joined for duty from the 62nd Division. Capt. W. COLGAN R.A.M.C. joined for duty from the 32 Stationary Hosp.	LENS MAP
"	30/9/17		Left POMMERA and entrained at MONDICOURT. Detrained at HOUPLINES (Sheet 27 - to 17. Sheet 27 + 23.)	
OUDERDOM (Sheet 28)		Noon	(Control) at 9 A.M. Marched from HOUPLINES to OUDERDOM (sheet 28).	

2449 Wt. W14957/M90 750,000 1/16 J.B.C. & A. Forms/C.2118/12.

140/24+36

No. 21. 7.0.

COMMITTEE FOR THE
MEDICAL HISTORY OF THE WAR
Date —5 NOV. 1917

Army Form C. 2118.

WAR DIARY
or
INTELLIGENCE SUMMARY
(Erase heading not required.)

Vol 33

21st FIELD AMBULANCE
7th DIVISION

Place	Date	Hour	Summary of Events and Information	Remarks and references to Appendices
OUDERDOM	1.9.17		Received two motors from the 9nd S.A. Belgs to move the Ambulance to the SPEENVOORD = near HAZEBROUCK	Sheet 27-28 1,2,3,000
			Left OUDERDOM at 5 p.m. and marched to (Traps 27 K 27 A.B.3)	
Traps 27 K.27 A.B.3.	2.9.17		Capt V. Colgin proceeded to the 21st Division for duty.	
			Capt. J.T. Lloyd joined for duty from B Corps Sigs Park	
			Capt. Mackay sick had sector & proceeded from No 3 Canadian Stat. Hosp.	
Traps 27 N.30 B.1.B	3.9.17		Marched to N.30 B.1.B Traps 27 1.20,000	
	6.9.17		Capt J.T. Lloyd proceeded on temps duty to No O/c 2 Divisno	
	8.9.17		Capt. A.F. READDIE rejoined for duty from the 2Lt. Manchester.	
HAUT. ARQUES	13.9.17		Marched to HAUT ARQUES (S.10.C.3.D)	HAZEBROUCK S.A.xxxii 2
	14.9.17		Capt F.S. Carson rejoined for duty from the 2D H.A.C.	
	15.9.17		Marched to LA WATTINE	
LA WATTINE	16.9.17		A.D.M.S. visited the Ambulance	
	20.9.17		Capt. J.T. Lloyd rejoined for duty from the 2" QUEENS. Received instructions from the A.D.M.S. I have took to a practice attack by the 7" Division on the 24. 25 + 26.9.17. This was to be taken part in the attack on the 22, + and	

WAR DIARY
or
INTELLIGENCE SUMMARY

(Erase heading not required.)

Army Form C. 2118.

Instructions regarding War Diaries and Intelligence Summaries are contained in F. S. Regs., Part II. and the Staff Manual respectively. Title Pages will be prepared in manuscript.

21st FIELD AMBULANCE
7th DIVISION

Place	Date	Hour	Summary of Events and Information	Remarks and references to Appendices
LA WATTINE	26/9/17		Took part in operative attack by the 7th Division. Established an A.D.S. at BARBINGHEM. Main Dressing Stn. at BARBINGHEM.	Ref. Map HAZEBROUCK S.A. 1/100,000
	27/9/17		Left LA WATTINE and marched to BUENE WAR QUEN	
BUENE WAR QUEN	28/9/17	3.30 AM	Marched to ARQUES and entrained without transport, detraining at ADEELE, and marched to ST HUBERSHOEK. The transport marched by road, stopping the night 28 9 17, 2½ mls at STAPLE, arriving the morning 29/9/17.	
ST HUBERSHOEK	29/9/17		A.D.M.S. visited the new location. Dist. 70/30/17/4m.	
	30/9/17		Received instructions from the F.D.M.S. to take over EDDE BIENFAISANCE on the 1st Oct. Rev.	

2/10/17.

[signatures]
O.C. 21st Field Amb.

140/2499

No. 21. 7.a.

COMMITTEE FOR THE
MEDICAL HISTORY OF THE WAR
Date −8 DEC. 1917

11

WAR DIARY
or
INTELLIGENCE SUMMARY

Army Form C. 2118.

21 3rd Aust V.C. 34

Place	Date	Hour	Summary of Events and Information	Remarks and references to Appendices
YPRES Ecole de BIENFAISANCE Ypres-Menin Road.	1/10/17		Marched to the YPRES-MENIN road and took over the ECOLE de BIENFAISANCE from Capt MEAGHER 22nd F.A. Received instructions to take in all Stretcher cases from the 5th - 7th and 21st Divisions. The three Divisions on the Capt O'REILLY forward road to take Red the 9th Army posts. A.D.S. at HOOGE CRATER, Relay Posts at HOOGE TUNNEL J.13.a.2.8. CLAPHAM JUNCTION J.13.c.8.8. - GLENCORSE WOOD J.14.b.4.B and POLYGON WOOD J.9.6.4.B. R.A.P.'s 1st BUTTE J.10.A.3.B. Line forward via POLYGON and GLENCORSE WOOD. CLAPHAM Junction, HOOGE TUNNEL to HOOGE CRATER thence all the wounded were evacuated via Motor Ambulances + taken into the ECOLE de BIEN FAISANCE YPRES-MENIN Road. Car Rendezvous established at the BIRR Cross Roads on the YPRES MENIN Road. Capt F.S. LARSON posted in M/C to A.D.S. HOOGE CRATER. All walking wounded are to be sent to WOODCOTE House on the YPRES ZILLEBEKE Road. The following were non mortal wounded No 43183 Pte KILLEEN, No 41775 Pte RADFORD No. 2995 Pte JAMIESON, No 40190 Pte BURNS F. A.D.M.S. visited the Dressing Station. Established men on duties at the ECOLE for Stretcher bearers A.C. Visited HOOGE CRATER	Ref MAP Sheet 28/1/20,000 N.W. N.E.

WAR DIARY or INTELLIGENCE SUMMARY

Army Form C. 2118.

Place	Date	Hour	Summary of Events and Information	Remarks and references to Appendices
YPRES ECOLE de BIENFAISANCE YPRES-MENIN Road	2/10/17		Number of cars admitted from 6.A.M on the 1st inst to 6.A.M on the 2nd inst 870. The following cases this record amongst the known NO 8331 Pte Nicholson J.F. killed in action. No. 8300 Pte SHERMAN wounded & returned.	Ref Ypres Sheet 28/7/20000 W.W. NE
"	3/10/17		Number of cars admitted from 6.A.M on the 2nd inst to 6.A.M on the 3rd inst 785 of which 214 O.R. Capt Macevay posted to Clapham Junction in relief of Capt O'Reilly who on leaving relieved myself at the Ecole. 7 /w A.D.M.S. visited the Dressing Station.	
"	4/10/17		The 5th & 21st Division in march-ul at 5.20 A.M. 3rd inst to 6.A.M 4th inst 214. The following casualties amongst from 6.A.M. No 75363 Pte WILLIAMS W. killed in action. No 216440 Pte FERNIE. No 10103 Pte MARSH E. No 72350 Pte WOODWARD A. No D317 Pte TURTON F. No 108-609 Pte EDWARDS R. No 31930 Pte HALL G. No 58861 Pte PIERSON R. No 90242 Pte CONNOR J. No 101738 Pte Wounded. Capts L.D. BUCKLEY & GARDINER Joined for duty. Party from Pte 28 2) F.A. Between 7+800 walking cases were evacuated from the Ecole by horse lorries and 44 1/2 ambulance drawn. D.D.M.6 7 the I.Corps visited the Dressing Station. The M.A.C. had 68 Motor Ambulances at the room for the CLS. Number of cases admitted from 6.A.M 3rd inst to 6.A.M 4th inst 10 Off 203 O.R.	

2449. Wt. W.4957/M90. 750,000 1/16 J.B.C. & A. Forms/C.2118/12

WAR DIARY or INTELLIGENCE SUMMARY

Army Form C. 2118.

Place	Date	Hour	Summary of Events and Information	Remarks and references to Appendices
YPRES - Ecole etc BIENFAISANCE	5/10/17		No German Artillery fire from 6 A.M. until 6 B.A.M. 5 until 11 B Off 5=99. OR +33 Germans. Rifl. Profs. The Artillery Barrage received Manged the Forward. No 10610 Pte DOUTHWAITE. R.E. Shrot 28/1/17 ccos No 6000 Pte DEAN. T.A. No 11491 Pte SALES. G. No 8077 Pte 4/4L MITCHELL. A. No 31041 - NWN.E. Pte COX.V. and No 9404 Pte PARKINSON. Vul. Wounds. Capt 2Lloyd proceeded to Mo/c 210 Manchesters to Shar Bight - REID Killed in action. A.D.M.S. visited the Dressing station	
"	6/10/17		Number of Cases admitted from 6 A.M. to 6 A.M. 6 April 160 Off. 373 O.R. The following Casualties were enemy of the forward. No 789425 Pte SIMMONDS. C. Chief of Barrack. No 9899 Pte NEATES. W No 6708 Pte SANSAN. C. No 35787 BELL. A.T. No 3361 Pte Cooper V. Killed in action No 78820 Pte SHEARIN. VW. No 102991 SMITH. I. No 8010 Pte SMITH. V.R. No 8141 Pte GERMAN. + No 65.08 Pte SUMMERS - GREEN No 35/46 Pte MATTHEWS.L. Wounded No 9596 Pte COOPER. F. Killed in action.	
"	7/10/17		Number of cases admitted from 6 th to 6 April - 6 A.M. 7 April 15 Off. 238. OR + 3 Germans. The following Casualties received Injury by the Enemy. No 9262 Ql. M. HIROM. H.N.T. No 25205 Pte EDMONDS. R. + No 812 Pte CONNAL. D. Wounded + remain by for duty.	

WAR DIARY
or
INTELLIGENCE SUMMARY

(Erase heading not required.)

Army Form C. 2118.

Place	Date	Hour	Summary of Events and Information	Remarks and references to Appendices
ECOLE de BIENFAISANE YPRES-MENIN ROAD	8/10/17		Transfer submitted from 6 A.M. on the 7th and 8 8 A.M. on the 8th instant 41 O.R. 88 O.R. + 9 Germans. Received instructions that 1st Division had taken over at 3 P.M. on the 7th instant by Gen 21st Division. From J.5.b.2.0 to V.10.c.9.0 + were actively at 5.20 A.M. on the 8th inst, time that was to TC 23 Pte F.A. Arthur of uncertain B. wounded from the front line, D.5 km at the ECOLE de BIENFAISANE, J. wounded from the front line. No 9700 Pte NYE.E wounded & interred. The following Casualties occurred amongst the tamed [troops].	R.I. Corps Sheet 28N/20. OD N.W.N.E.
	9/10/17		Transfer submitted from 8 A.M. on the 8th inst, 2 8 A.M. on the 9th inst 5 O.R. 106 O.R. The following casualties occurred amongst the troops. No 575999 Pte Wilson W. wounded. No 74923 Pte Moore C.S. No 7271 Pte Dunning. C. No 10917 Pte Bunyard.H + No 31045 Pte Cook.F wounded.	
	10/10/17		Transfer submitted from 6 A.M. on the 9th inst 2 8 A.M. on the 10th inst 15 Off/147. O.R. R.O.W. Received instructions from the R.O. to B. [moved] over the ECOLE de BIENFAISANE B this OC 70 L F.A on the 11th inst. The following Casualties occurred amongst the troops No 31989 Pte Wilson W. + No 10655 L/C. HUMPHREYS J.A. and No 6596 Pte MARTIN H.C. and 6STFARM.A.Y from dust + injury	

Army Form C. 2118.

WAR DIARY
or
INTELLIGENCE SUMMARY

(Erase heading not required.)

Instructions regarding War Diaries and Intelligence Summaries are contained in F.S. Regs., Part II. and the Staff Manual respectively. Title Pages will be prepared in manuscript.

Place	Date	Hour	Summary of Events and Information	Remarks and references to Appendices
ECOLE YPRES-MENIN Road	11/10/17		Number admitted from B.W.M. on the 10th inst. to B.9.P.M. on the 11th inst 15 Offrs + 147 O.Rs + 1 P.O.W. Total number admitted from 12 Noon on the 1st inst to 8 A.M. on the 11th inst 132 Offrs 2145 O.R. + 51 P.O.W. Evacuated to 2 B. Stationary Amb 2 BRD Hunted Q on the Dressing Station to Bt. 70 F.A. Evac: transed to 2 Evg Coten	HAZEBROUCK E.42.5.A.
ZEVECOTEN	12/10/17		Ambulance remains closed. A.D.M.S. visited the Ambulance. Lt. VANCE N.Z.O.R.C. joined for duty from the X Corps Reinforcement Camp.
"	13/10/17		Capt. A.F. READDIE proceeded on temp. duty in M.O i/c 22 Bde R.F.A.
"	14/10/17		Received instructions from the A.D.M.S. to move on the 20th inst. to BERTHEN
"	18/10/17		Marched to BERTHEN. Ambulance now opened closed.
BERTHEN	19/10/17		Received instructions from the A.D.M.S. to take over the DIVISIONAL Rest Station at CHIPPEWA CAMP Sheet 27.
	22/10/17		N.5.A.B.B. (Sheet 27) from the 22nd F.A. on the 23rd inst.
	23/10/17		Capt. D. Frew + Capt. L. MACKAY proceeded this day to S.C.L. Ch... in... moved into 102 the Div Rest Stn 62 N. 6.B.B.D. L.Cpl. S. Carson M.C. proceeded on temp duty as D. O i/c 2 B. Stationary.

2449 Wt. W14957/M90 750,000 1/16 J.B.C. & A. Forms/C.2118/12.

Army Form C. 2118.

WAR DIARY
or
INTELLIGENCE SUMMARY

(Erase heading not required.)

Instructions regarding War Diaries and Intelligence Summaries are contained in F. S. Regs., Part II. and the Staff Manual respectively. Title Pages will be prepared in manuscript.

Place	Date	Hour	Summary of Events and Information	Remarks and references to Appendices
BERTHEN - No.6.A.R.P. Sheet 27.	24/10/17		Received 2nd Lieut CHIPP en a Camp N.6.A.R.P. Capt. McAFEE joined for duty. Lieut Jones left 2º Divno. A.D.M.S. visited 1st Res/Stn. Received orders from 1st A.D.Sinc. Division to be attached + move over the opening of the 22º F.A.	Sheet 27. 1/us.oos
	29/10/17		Capt. A.F. READDIE reported for duty from the 22nd Bde R.F.A. Received instructions from the A.D.M.S. for the joining ofMessrs Two Officers from each Field Division to proceed on the 30th ins to EBBLINGHEM. The transport to proceed by Road	
EBBLINGHEM	30/10/17		Capt. D. MARR + Capt MACKAY with Advant 1st Section took over charge of the Rest Section. Capt. O'REILLY marched the transport to EBBLINGHEM. Capt A.F READDIE rendezvoused the personnel at OUDERDOM 6.15-10.15 A.M for EBBLINGHEM	HAZEBROUCK S.A.ed 2.
	31/10/17		Capt. C.J. O'REILLY. M.C and Capt G.R.J MACKAY M.C left Mortuvined to take its Water Ministry Line. Capt. L.S. CARSON M.C. reported for duty from the 2º Divno. Capt M.C AFLEE reported the 2º QUEENS.	

2/11/17

[signature]
Lt Col M.G.R.C
O. 2/1st F.A

40/578

COMMITTEE FOR THE
MEDICAL HISTORY OF THE WAR
Date   17 JAN. 1918

No. 21. + a.

WAR DIARY or INTELLIGENCE SUMMARY

Army Form C. 2118.

Place	Date	Hour	Summary of Events and Information	Remarks and references to Appendices
EBBLINGHEM	1/11/17		Capt D. M. MARR proceeded to No 17 CCS for duty	HAZEBROUCK SA sh 2
"	2/11/17		Capt B.R. MACKAY returned from the Capts Rest Stn CALAIS ANIA CAMP to the 133rd FA and rejoined H.Q. for duty	Ref. Trench map Calais sh 13
"	5/11/17		Lt WILLIAMS proceeded on temp duty to No 11 CCS	Hazebrouck sh 15 A
"	8/11/17		The ambulance is attached for rations for the King of the BELGIANS	
ECQUIRE	9/11/17		Marched to ECQUIRE. The ambulance formed H.Q. at B.A.Th.	LENS sh II.
SENLECQUES	10/11/17	10.6 M	Marched to SENLECQUES.	
ECQUIRE	11/11/17	10.6 M	Capt J.D. Jacobson joined for duty from the 8th Div. Lt VANCE rejoined from No 11 CCS. Marched to ECQUIRE. Lt Br. VANCE to S.A.(R) was attached to the 39th Div for duty	
FRUGES	12/11/17	B.A.Th.	Capt S.Th. POWELL joined Lieut J.A. LEES joined for duty from the 19th Division. Marched to FRUGES	
	13/11/17	B.A.Th.	Capt J. ADAM joined for duty from the 19th Division and Lieut. H. WIDDAS from the 30th Division. Lt WILLIAMS rejoined for duty to the 19th Division	
BOYAVAL	14/11/17	6.30 A.M	Marched to BOYAVAL	
	15/11/17		Capt Jacobson proceeded as M.O.i/c vii Div Train	
"	19/11/17	3.30 A.M	proceeded to ANVIN Sta to Entrain Entrained col.	

Army Form C. 2118.

WAR DIARY
or
INTELLIGENCE SUMMARY

(Erase heading not required.)

Place	Date	Hour	Summary of Events and Information	Remarks and references to Appendices
LEGNAGO (ITALY)	25/11/17	4.30 p.m.	Detrained 6/h. 8½ days journey by rail. Billetted the unit for the nig. 16 in LEGNAGO	Ref Maps VERONA-PADOVA F° 12 FERRARA F° 20 Scale 1/200,000
ASIGLIANO	26/11/17	9 6.m.	Marched to ASIGLIANO	
CAMPIGLIA	27/11/17	9 a.m.	Marched to CAMPIGLIA	
VILLAGA	28/11/17	10 a.m.	Marched to VILLAGA	
	29/11/17		Capt POWELL was evacuated (sick) to No 38 C.C.S. A.D.M.S. inspected the Ambulance	
CAMPODORO	30/11/17	8.30 a.m.	Marched to CAMPODORO	

In the Field
3rd Dec 1917.

[signature]
Lt.Col R.A.M.C.
O/C 21st F.A.